*Oracle Press*™

Using R to Unlock the Value of Big Data

Big Data Analytics with Oracle R Enterprise and Oracle R Connector for Hadoop

Mark Hornick

Tom Plunkett

New York   Chicago   San Francisco
Athens   London   Madrid   Mexico City
Milan   New Delhi   Singapore   Sydney   Toronto

Using R to Unlock the Value of Big Data: Big Data Analytics with Oracle R Enterprise and Oracle R Connector for Hadoop

ISBN   978-0-07-182438-5
MHID   0-07-182438-3

Sponsoring Editor
Paul Carlstroem

Editorial Supervisor
Janet Walden

Project Manager
Nidhi Chopra, Cenveo
Publisher Services

Acquisitions Coordinator
Amanda Russell

Technical Editors
Jean-Pierre Dijcks
Dan McClary

Copy Editor
Margaret Berson

Proofreader
Claire Splan

Production Supervisor
Jean Bodeaux

Composition
Cenveo Publisher Services

Illustration
Cenveo Publisher Services

Art Director, Cover
Jeff Weeks

Cover Designer
Pattie Lee

Contents

About the Authors

Mark Hornick is a Director in the Oracle Database Advanced Analytics group focusing on Oracle R Enterprise (ORE), Oracle R Connector for Hadoop (ORCH), and Oracle R Distribution (ORD). He also works with internal and external customers in the application of R for scalable applications in Oracle Database, Exadata, and the Big Data Appliance, also engaging in SAS-to-R conversion and performance benchmarking. Mark is co-author of *Java Data Mining: Strategy, Standard, and Practice*. He joined Oracle's Data Mining Technologies group in 1999 through the acquisition of Thinking Machines Corp. Mark was a founding member of and currently serves as an Oracle Advisor to the IOUG Business Intelligence Warehousing and Analytics (BIWA) SIG. He has conducted training sessions on R, ORE, and ORCH in the US, EMEA, and APAC, and has presented at conferences including Oracle OpenWorld, Collaborate, BIWA Summit, and the R user conference useR! Mark holds a bachelor's degree from Rutgers University and a master's degree from Brown University, both in computer science.

Tom Plunkett is a Senior Sales Consultant with Oracle. Tom also teaches graduate-level computer science courses for Virginia Tech as an adjunct instructor and distance learning instructor. Tom helped win several industry awards for a big data project that Oracle and the Frederick National Laboratory for Cancer Research collaborated on to analyze relationships between genomes and cancer subtypes, including the 2012 Government Big Data Solution Award, ACT-IAC finalist for best pilot/start-up project, and was nominated for a 2013 Computer World Honor Award for Innovation. Tom has spoken internationally at over forty conferences on the subject of Big Data since leading a team that won a Big Data project from the Office of the Secretary of Defense in 2009. Tom is the lead author of several books, including *Oracle Big Data Handbook* and *Oracle Exalogic Elastic Cloud Handbook*. Previously, Tom worked for IBM and practiced patent law for Fliesler Meyer. Tom has a BA and a JD from George Mason University, and an MS in computer science from Virginia Tech.

Thanks are due to Jean-Pierre Dijcks and Dan McClary for their technical editing and input during the writing of this book.

Using R to Unlock the Value of Big Data

Big Data Analytics with Oracle R Enterprise
and Oracle R Connector for Hadoop

The focus of this book is on analyzing data with R while making it scalable using Oracle's R technologies. Initial sections provide an introduction to open source R and issues with traditional R and database interaction. Subsequent sections cover Oracle's strategic R offerings: Oracle R Enterprise 1.3, Oracle R Distribution, ROracle, and Oracle R Connector for Hadoop 2.0.

Oracle's R product offerings complement Oracle's other products in the Big Data space. This book is based on an expanded and updated chapter from the companion book, *Oracle Big Data Handbook*, which provides comprehensive details on Oracle's Big Data strategy and product offerings. Among other changes, this work includes a section of exercises that is not contained within *Oracle Big Data Handbook*.

We will start with what open source R is and how it relates to Oracle products.

Introduction to Open Source R

R is an open-source language and environment for statistical computing and data visualization, supporting data manipulation and transformations, as well as conventional and more sophisticated graphics. With millions of users worldwide, R is widely taught in universities, and increasingly used by data analysts and data scientists in enterprise environments.

R is a statistics language similar to SAS or SPSS. It is powerful in that users can accomplish much computation with minimal specification. It is extensible in that users can write their own functions and packages, leveraging object-oriented and functional programming language constructs. An R *package* is a collection of typically related functions, data, and compiled code, organized using a well-defined format. R itself is organized as a set of packages.

User-defined packages enable automating analysis and can be used by the individual, shared within the organization, or published to the Comprehensive R Archive Network (CRAN) for sharing with the R community. R has a wide range of statistics and data visualization capabilities. While the default arguments are often sufficient to get started, there are plenty of *knobs* to customize or fine-tune results.

Perhaps one aspect that has also helped R's adoption is that it is easy to install and use, and it is free—downloadable from the R project Web site. Consider downloading and installing R from the CRAN Web site today.

CRAN, Packages, and Task Views

R package growth has been exponential, with thousands of contributors, and that trend continues. Today, there are over four thousand packages in the R ecosystem. Each package provides specialized functionality, in areas such as bioinformatics, financial market analysis, and numerous others. Table 1 shows CRAN Task Views, which are areas of concentration for sets of related R packages. Each Task View Web page provides a description of the packages supporting that area.

Table 2 depicts a sampling of content available in the Machine Learning and Statistical Learning task view. While Oracle Database provides a rich set of in-database

Task View	Description
Bayesian	Bayesian Inference
ChemPhys	Chemometrics and Computational Physics
ClinicalTrials	Clinical Trial Design, Monitoring, and Analysis
Cluster	Cluster Analysis and Finite Mixture Models
DifferentialEquations	Differential Equations
Distributions	Probability Distributions
Econometrics	Computational Econometrics
Environmetrics	Analysis of Ecological and Environmental Data
ExperimentalDesign	Design of Experiments (DoE) and Analysis of Experimental Data
Finance	Empirical Finance
Genetics	Statistical Genetics
Graphics	Graphic Displays and Dynamic Graphics and Graphic Devices and Visualization
HighPerformanceComputing	High-Performance and Parallel Computing with R
MachineLearning	Machine Learning and Statistical Learning
MedicalImaging	Medical Image Analysis
Multivariate	Multivariate Statistics
NaturalLanguageProcessing	Natural Language Processing
OfficialStatistics	Official Statistics and Survey Methodology
Optimization	Optimization and Mathematical Programming
Pharmacokinetics	Analysis of Pharmacokinetic Data
Phylogenetics	Phylogenetics, Especially Comparative Methods
Psychometrics	Psychometric Models and Methods
ReproducibleResearch	Reproducible Research
Robust	Robust Statistical Methods
SocialSciences	Statistics for the Social Sciences
Spatial	Analysis of Spatial Data
SpatioTemporal	Handling and Analyzing Spatio-Temporal Data
Survival	Survival Analysis
TimeSeries	Time Series Analysis
gR	gRaphical Models in R

TABLE 1.   *CRAN Task Views*

Algorithm Class	Packages
Neural Networks	**nnet** Single-hidden-layer neural network **RSNNS** Stuttgart Neural Network Simulator
Recursive Partitioning	**rpart** Regression, classification, and survival analysis for CART-like trees **RWeka** Partitioning algorithms available in Weka, for example, C4.5 and M5 **Cubist** Rule-based models with linear regression models in terminal leaves **C50** C5.0 classification trees, rule-based models, and boosted versions
Random Forests	**randomForest** Reference implementation of the random forest algorithm **ipred** Bagging for regression, classification, and survival analysis as well as bundling **randomSurvivalForest** Random forest algorithm for censored data **quantregForest** Quantile regression forests
Boosting	**gbm** Various forms of gradient boosting **bst** Hinge-loss optimized by boosting implementation **GAMBoost** Fit-generalized additive models by a boosting algorithm
Support Vector Machines and Kernel Methods	**e1071** Svm() interface to the LIBSVM library **kernlab** Implements a flexible framework for kernel learning **klaR** SVMlight implementation for one-against-all classification
Bayesian Methods	**BayesTree** Bayesian Additive Regression Trees **tgp** Bayesian nonstationary, semiparametric nonlinear regression
Optimization Using Genetic Algorithms	**rgp** Optimization routines **rgenoud** Optimization routines
Association Rules	**arules** A priori algorithm with efficient data structures for sparse data **Eclat** Mining frequent itemsets, maximal frequent itemsets, closed frequent itemsets, association rules

TABLE 2.   *Machine Learning and Statistical Learning Task View*

algorithms, there are others that may be required by a project for which open source R adds value.

GUIs and IDEs

Although R comes with a default integrated development environment (IDE), there are many other IDEs to choose from. For example, one is a third-party, open source IDE called RStudio, which has a more finished look to it as well as some convenient features. Note, however, that Oracle has no affiliation with RStudio and does not provide support for RStudio.

As shown in Figure 1, users can view and edit R scripts in the upper left-hand frame, and then select a portion of an R script to execute by clicking Run. In the figure, the R script loads the `igraph` package and then accesses online documentation for `igraph`. Documentation appears in the Help tab (not shown).

One can switch between plots, packages, help, and even navigate to previously accessed help and generated plots. In the example, a *Barabasi game*, or small-world graph generated by the Barabasi algorithm, has been initialized. Here, the Barabasi algorithm produces a preferential attachment model with 100 nodes, which is then plotted with a `fruchterman.reingold` layout.

While RStudio is the top-ranked interface after the built-in R console, according to a 2011 KDNuggets survey, there are many others, such as R Commander and `rattle`. The package `Rcmdr`, which supports R Commander, is one of the oldest GUIs for R based on the `tcltk` package. R Commander takes, for example, the

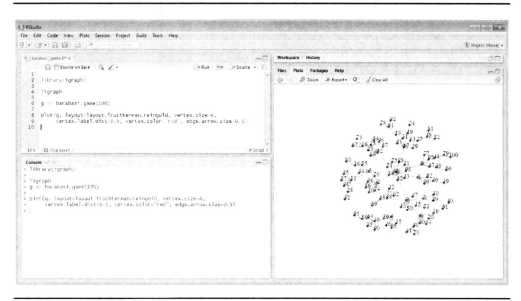

FIGURE 1.   *RStudio IDE*

most commonly used statistical functions and exposes them through a drop-down menu interface with dialogs that prompt the user for needed arguments. This enables users who are not familiar with programming but know what they want to accomplish to use R. The underlying code that is generated by R Commander can be exposed for further editing by the user.

The `rattle` (R Analytic Tool to Learn Easily) GUI provides a Gnome-based interface to data mining functionality in R—all without needing to know details of R programming. The `rattle` interface presents the user with the standard sequence of steps, or workflow, that an analyst would commonly go through to solve a data mining problem.

Both R Commander and `rattle` can be used within the standard R interface, or within RStudio.

Traditional R and Database Interaction vs. Oracle R Enterprise

Most enterprise data is stored in relational databases. As illustrated in Figure 2, a common way for data analysts to access data is through flat files. A request is made to a DBA who produces an extract and makes it available to the analyst. When completed, results consisting of predictive models, data scores, or other analytical results are exported to flat files for import back to the database. From there, results can be accessed by enterprise applications.

As is commonly experienced, this approach introduces significant latency for data access, especially if the correct data was not provided the first time or the

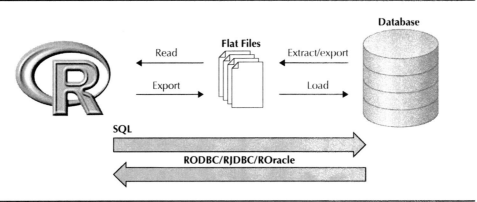

FIGURE 2. *Aspects of traditional R and database interaction*

analyst determined that different or additional data was required. This can result in multiple iterations before the analyst gets the needed set of tables or columns, adding hours, days, or weeks to a project. In addition, when using data extracts, which are often stored on local user hard drives, enterprises need to address data backup, recovery, and security.

For those users familiar with SQL, there are R packages for direct database access, for example, RODBC, RJDBC, and ROracle. While this type of access is an improvement over flat file exchange, it requires a paradigm shift between R and SQL. Users must think in terms of SQL queries, not R objects, and have the package map data from tables into data.frames, and vice versa, which may or may not have the semantics required by the user.

When it comes time to deploy an analytics-based solution involving R, application developers may resort to a carefully scripted cron job to operationalize the process of extracting data, running the R script, and returning results. However, this can produce a complex architecture and more moving parts that must be tracked and managed. Moreover, the R scripts and any reusable R objects written out to files must be managed at the file system level as part of production deployment. To avoid some of these issues, an application architect may require the results of analysis, such as R models, to be translated into SQL, C, or Java, for inclusion in applications. This translation process is tedious and error-prone and can result in significant delay between model creation and production deployment.

Another concern for enterprise data is that R is a client and interpreter bundled together as a single executable. As a single-user tool, despite recent improvements, much of its functionality is not multithreaded or parallel. Moreover, it cannot generally leverage CPU capacity on a user's desktop without the use of special packages and coding.

R also normally requires the data it operates on to be loaded into memory. There are CRAN packages that support out-of-memory data, such as those related to the bigmemory package, but these may still require data extracts and as such would not alleviate enterprise concerns over backup, recovery, security, and overall application complexity. In general, analyzing enterprise-sized data sets may not be possible if the data cannot be loaded into memory. Even if loading some larger data sets is possible, R's call-by-value semantics means that as data flows into functions, for each function invocation, a copy of the data may be made. As a result, memory can quickly be exhausted when trying to analyze data.

To address the needs of enterprises for advanced analytics, Oracle R Enterprise enhances open source R in several ways. First, it allows R users to analyze and manipulate data in Oracle Database through R, transparently. For base R functionality, users write code as though working with data.frames, but the R functions are overloaded to execute in the database on database data—transparently translated to SQL. This leverages the database as a high-performance and scalable compute engine. With this *Transparency Layer*, users experience reduced latency, reduced application complexity, and increased performance and security, while operating on bigger data (not limited by the memory constraint of R). In all, SQL knowledge is no longer required to manipulate database data.

Oracle R Enterprise also enables users to take advantage of data-parallel and task-parallel execution through Oracle Database. This *Embedded R Execution* enables "lights out" execution of R scripts. The R scripts developed to support database applications can be stored and managed in the database R script repository. Embedded R Execution can be accessed by both R and SQL interfaces. The SQL interface enables working seamlessly with database applications and facilitates integration with OBIEE RPDs and dashboards and Oracle BI Publisher documents. Open source CRAN packages can be installed at the database server R engine and used in embedded R scripts.

Oracle R Enterprise exposes in-database predictive analytics algorithms seamlessly through R, that is, algorithms from Oracle Data Mining and Oracle R Enterprise (ORE)-provided algorithms including stepwise linear regression and artificial neural networks. To enhance predictive model performance, R models can be used to score data in-database, effectively translating the native R model into SQL. Executing the corresponding SQL leverages Oracle Database as a powerful compute engine.

One of the features unique to Oracle R Enterprise is how R scripts are dynamically integrated into the SQL language. As discussed in the section "Embedded R Execution," users can define R scripts, store them in Oracle Database, and invoke them by name within SQL statements.

Lastly, when it comes to operationalizing analytics results, often seen as the killer of applications projects, Oracle R Enterprise integrates R into the IT software stack, without requiring additional components, like `Rserve`. By making R functions accessible from SQL, database and enterprise application developers can readily leverage the results of the analytics side of the house without complex plumbing, recoding, or mapping of results to database tables.

Oracle's Strategic R Offerings

A key goal for Oracle is to deliver enterprise-level advanced analytics based on the R environment. To enable this, Oracle provides Oracle R Enterprise, Oracle R Distribution, an enhanced open source `ROracle` package for database connectivity and, in terms of Big Data on Hadoop, Oracle R Connector for Hadoop.

Oracle R Enterprise

Oracle R Enterprise (ORE) is a component of the Oracle Advanced Analytics option to Oracle Database Enterprise Edition. ORE eliminates R's memory constraints by working on data directly in the database. By leveraging in-database analytics, ORE augments R with both scalability and high performance. Moreover, ORE provides a comprehensive, database-centric environment covering the full range of analytical processes in R where R users can rapidly develop and deploy R scripts that work on database data. Being integrated with Oracle Database, ORE can execute R scripts through the database—leveraging Oracle Database as a high-performance computing (HPC) environment.

The integration with the SQL language enables invoking R scripts from SQL to support enterprise applications. This also enables Oracle BI Publisher documents and OBIEE dashboards to access analytics results produced by R, including graphs and images. R users can also leverage the latest R algorithms and contributed packages.

From a high-level architectural perspective, Figure 3 depicts the R workspace console (IDE) where users interactively execute R scripts. ORE overloads R functions that normally operate on `data.frames` and pushes down their execution to Oracle Database, where transformations and statistical computations are performed on database tables. ORE introduces `ore.frame` objects that serve as proxies for database tables and views.

In Oracle Database, the statistics engine consists of native database functionality, such as those that leverage SQL and the various DBMS packages, as well as enhancements specific to ORE. As noted earlier, results from ORE can be exposed through OBIEE dashboards and Web Services-based applications.

Three key points are: ORE requires little or no change to the R user experience, the database provides the ability to scale to large data sets, and analytics results can be embedded in operational or production systems—supporting areas of interactive development, production deployment, and end-user consumption.

Figure 4 depicts an OBIEE dashboard where the graph is produced by invoking a parameterized R script for execution through the database. As shown in the figure, one can select data subsets and customize graph characteristics, such as orientation, color, and box plot width. When the user clicks Apply (hidden in the figure), the

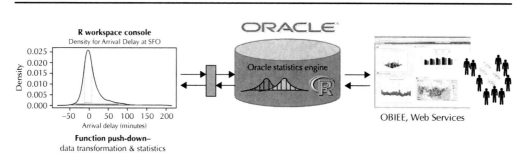

FIGURE 3. *High-level architectural perspective of Oracle R Enterprise*

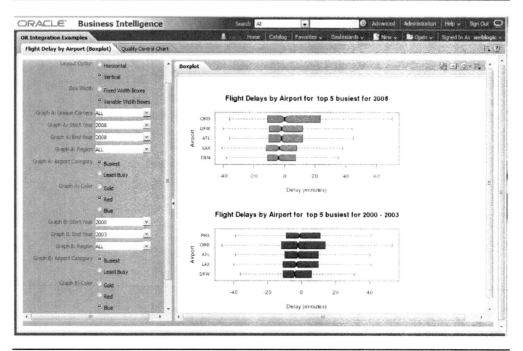

FIGURE 4. *ORE integrated with OBIEE dashboard for dynamic, parameterized graph generation*

request is sent to the database for execution by a database server R engine. The graph is returned for display in the dashboard and can be represented as a base 64 encoding of the PNG image as part of an XML string, or as a PNG BLOB table column. R scripts can compute structured results for display in dashboard tables, as well as to generate sophisticated graphics. Open source CRAN packages that perform statistical calculations and generate graphs can be installed at the database server R engine for generating dashboard graphs in a similar manner.

Oracle R Distribution

Oracle R Distribution, a free download from Oracle, is Oracle's redistribution of open source R, with enhancements to dynamically load high-performance math libraries from Intel, AMD, and Solaris if they are present on the machine. (Note, however, that these libraries, such as Intel's MKL, are not included with Oracle R Distribution and may need to be licensed separately.) High-performance libraries include core math functions such as sparse solvers, fast Fourier transforms, vector math, and others that transparently increase the performance of R functions relying on them.

Oracle provides support for Oracle R Distribution for customers of Oracle R Enterprise, Big Data Appliance, or Oracle Linux—so Oracle stands behind the R software. The lack of a major corporate sponsor has made some companies leery of fully adopting R. With Oracle R Distribution, enterprise customers have greater confidence in adopting R enterprise-wide. Oracle R Distribution is available and supported on Oracle Enterprise Linux, AIX, and Solaris.

ROracle

The database interface driver `ROracle` is an open source R package now maintained by Oracle, providing high-performance connectivity between R and Oracle Database. Oracle R Enterprise uses `ROracle` for connectivity between R and Oracle Database. `ROracle` has been re-engineered using the Oracle Call Interface (OCI) with optimizations and bug fixes made available to the open source community. `ROracle` implements the database interface (DBI) package definitions.

Oracle R Connector for Hadoop

Oracle R Connector for Hadoop—one of the components of the Oracle Big Data Connectors—provides an R interface to a Hadoop cluster, allowing R users to access and manipulate data in Hadoop Distributed File System (HDFS), Oracle Database, and the file system. R users can write MapReduce functions using R and execute Hadoop jobs using a natural R interface. In addition, Oracle R Connector for Hadoop provides several native Hadoop-based analytics techniques as part of the package. Data stored in Hive can be accessed and manipulated through a transparency layer similar to that of ORE.

Oracle R Enterprise: Next-Level View

From the perspective of a collaborative execution model, Oracle R Enterprise (ORE) leverages three layers of computational engines, as depicted in Figure 5. The first layer is the R engine on a user's desktop, where users work interactively on database data and perform local post-processing of results provided by the database. The Transparency Layer allows R users to access database tables and views via proxy objects. These proxy objects of type `ore.frame` are a subclass of `data.frame`. Through function overloading, invoking functions on `ore.frame` objects results in generated SQL that is executed in the database.

The second compute engine is Oracle Database itself. Through the Transparency Layer, the SQL generated through R function invocation is executed in the database—taking advantage of query optimization, database parallelism, and

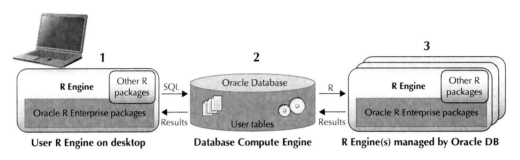

FIGURE 5.   *Computational engines supporting Oracle R Enterprise*

scalability. In vanilla R, a series of function invocations is executed sequentially, producing a result from each function. With ORE, the SQL generated through a series of functions can be stacked and not executed until an intermediate result is needed for subsequent computation, or the user requests the result. This allows the database query optimizer to optimize the stacked SQL prior to execution. When configured for parallelism, Oracle Database will automatically take advantage of multiple processors to execute SQL queries, which also applies to the SQL generated through the Transparency Layer. Scalability is achieved since data is not loaded into the client R engine prior to function invocation.

The third compute engine is composed of R engines spawned to execute on the database server machine, under the control of Oracle Database. By executing at the database server, data can be loaded to the R engine and written to the database more efficiently than between the R client and the database.

Embedded R Execution enables

■ Data and task parallelism

■ The return of rich XML or PNG image output

■ SQL access to R

■ Running parallel simulations

■ Use of third-party (CRAN) and custom packages at the database server

Oracle R Enterprise enables a simplified architecture, while eliminating the constraints of the client R engine, as shown in Figure 6. This architecture enables enterprises and data analysts to get even greater value from Oracle Database for advanced analytics by leveraging R with database scalability and performance. When combined with Oracle Exadata, these benefits are further amplified.

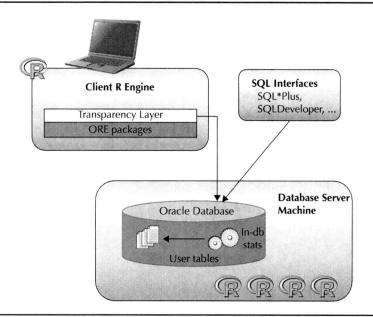

FIGURE 6. *Oracle R Enterprise architecture*

Once analysts complete their work, solution deployment is immediate. Traditionally, an analyst's results, such as predictive models, would be manually translated into SQL for in-database scoring against large data sets. With Oracle R Enterprise, the R scripts can be stored in the database R script repository and invoked by name, directly within SQL statements. In addition, R objects both intermediate and final can be store in a database R *datastore*, which is discussed in a later section.

Oracle R Enterprise Installation and Configuration

From a prerequisites standpoint, Oracle R Enterprise is supported on 64-bit Linux x86-64, Microsoft Windows, Solaris on both SPARC and x86, IBM AIX, as well as Oracle Exadata and SPARC SuperCluster. Check the Oracle R Enterprise documentation for the latest version of R supported. Oracle Database 11.2.0.3 or above is suggested, although earlier 11.2 releases are supported with a patch, as indicated in the ORE installation guide.

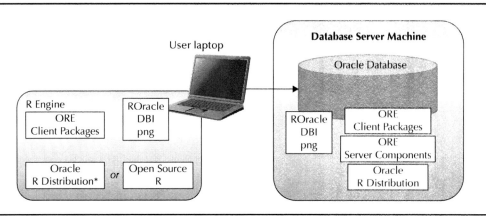

User laptop

FIGURE 7.   *ORE component packages and R engine configuration*

Figure 7 depicts ORE package and R engine configuration. Users first install R, either the Oracle R Distribution or open source R, on the client and server machines. ORE packages and supplemental packages (ROracle, DBI, and png) are then installed into R, both at the client and server. At the database server, ORE libraries (.so) are linked with Oracle Database.

When installing on Exadata, ORE packages and R must be installed on each Exadata node. The ORE package installation consists of the client packages shown in Table 3, along with the supplemental packages noted previously. See the *Oracle R Enterprise Installation and Administration Guide* for complete installation requirements and instructions.

ORE Package	Description
OREbase	Corresponds to R's base package
OREstats	Corresponds to R's stat package
OREgraphics	Corresponds to R's graphics package
OREeda	Exploratory data analysis package
OREdm	Exposes Oracle Data Mining algorithms
OREpredict	Enables scoring data in Oracle DB using R models
ORExml	Supports XML translation between R and Oracle Database

TABLE 3.   *ORE Packages*

Using Oracle R Enterprise

This section provides detailed examples using the ORE Transparency Layer, Embedded R Execution, and predictive analytics.

Transparency Layer

The Transparency Layer supports in-database data exploration, data preparation, and data analysis often en route to the application of predictive analytics, where users have access to a mix of in-database and open source R techniques.

Transparency means that for base R functionality, R users can write code as though working with R `data.frames` and then transparently have that code operate on database data, leveraging the database as a high-performance and scalable compute engine. R users do not need to learn a different programming paradigm or environment such as SQL to access and manipulate database data. They can operate on database data as though they were native R objects using R syntax. While `ore.frame` objects have been explicitly mentioned, ORE maps a range of primitive object types, for example, `ore.vector` and `ore.numeric`, to database data.

Transparency also means that for R scripts that leverage base R functionality, minimal change is required to work with database data. Internally, transparency means that R functions are transparently translated to SQL for in-database execution, gaining performance and scalability.

A major benefit of the Transparency Layer is that as R functions are translated to SQL, much of this SQL is *stacked*—not immediately executed, but accumulated. When a result is finally needed, either for a computation or for viewing by the user, the stacked SQL is executed. This allows the database to perform query optimization on that SQL. This is not possible in native R or even interactive one-off invocations of SQL where intermediate results are pulled back to the client.

Connecting to Oracle Database

To get started with the Transparency Layer, users first connect to an Oracle database that has ORE installed. As shown in Example 1, users check if already connected to a database using the function `is.ore.connected`. In this example, arguments to `ore.connect` specify the `"rquser"` schema with SID `"orcl"` on the local host. The password is specified in this example, but there are other options to avoid clear-text passwords.

Example 1:

```
if (!is.ore.connected())
   ore.connect("rquser", "orcl", "localhost", "password", all=TRUE)
ore.ls()
ore.disconnect()
ore.connect("rquser", "orcl", "localhost", "password")
ore.sync(table="MYDATA")
ore.attach()
```

The argument `all`, if set to `TRUE`, loads metadata about all the tables from the schema into `ore.frame` objects, making them available for use as R objects with the same name as the table—implicitly invoking the `ore.sync` and `ore.attach` functions. Invoking `ore.ls` lists the tables and views available as `ore.frame` objects in the attached schema. The function `ore.disconnect` will end an ORE session and free any temporary database objects. Connecting to the database without the `all` argument, the arguments to `ore.sync` in the example specify to load one table, `"MYDATA"`. If the schema contains a large number of tables that will not be used during the R session, this limits the number of `ore.frame` objects created (space) and the amount of time required to retrieve the corresponding table metadata. If a schema has thousands of tables, but only one or a few are needed, this savings can be significant. To make the objects available in the search path, the script invokes `ore.attach`. From here, users can do some interesting transformations and analysis on database data from R.

Data Manipulation

Example 2 illustrates two common database data manipulation operations: column and row selection. Projecting columns from a database table using an `ore.frame` object can be specified in a few ways:

- Specify the columns by name in a vector

- Provide a vector of column numbers

- Specify which columns to remove by using a minus sign

Example 2:

```
# Column selection
df <- ONTIME_S[,c("YEAR","DEST","ARRDELAY")]
class(df)
head(df)
head(ONTIME_S[,c(1,4,23)])
head(ONTIME_S[,-(1:22)])

#Row selection
df1 <- df[df$DEST=="SFO",]
```

```
class(df1)
df2 <- df[df$DEST=="SFO",c(1,3)]
df3 <- df[df$DEST=="SFO" | df$DEST=="BOS",1:3]
head(df1)
head(df2)
head(df3)
```

In the column selection R script, the first line selects YEAR, DEST, and ARRDELAY by column name. The next line selects three columns by column index, specified as a numeric vector. The following line removes columns 1 through 22 by putting a minus sign in front of the vector 1 through 22.

How does one remove a single column from a database table using SQL? Think about it. There are one thousand columns and the goal is to eliminate one column using a view. This will be discussed later.

To select rows from an ore.frame, specify a logical expression that is evaluated on each row. If the expression evaluates to true, that row is included in the result set. Notice that the column name is specified with the ore.frame object, as in df$DEST. If only DEST were specified, it would be an undefined variable at best, or refer to some other value or vector, likely producing an error when used in this scenario.

As in R, an arbitrarily complex logical expression can be specified with parentheses and logical operators for row selection. Row and column filtering can also be specified in the same statement. The first row selection example retrieves only rows where the destination contains "SFO." The second example includes the same rows, but retrieves only columns 1 and 3. The following example filters flights with a destination of "SFO" or "BOS," and takes columns 1, 2, and 3.

The results from the row selection code are shown in Listing 1. The first six rows of each result are shown using the overloaded head function. The function head works on ore.frame objects and retrieves table data from the database.

Listing 1   *Column and row selection results*

```
R> # Column selection
R> df <- ONTIME_S[,c("YEAR","DEST","ARRDELAY")]
R> class(df)
[1] "ore.frame"
attr(,"package")
[1] "OREbase"
R> head(df)
  YEAR DEST ARRDELAY
1 1987  MSP      4
2 1987  SJC      6
3 1987  OAK      7
4 1987  PHX      9
5 1987  CLT      0
6 1987  CVG      4
```

```
R> head(ONTIME_S[,c(1,4,23)])
  YEAR DAYOFMONTH TAXIOUT
1 1987          1     NA
2 1987          1     NA
3 1987          1     NA
4 1987          1     NA
5 1987          1     NA
6 1987          1     NA
R> head(ONTIME_S[,-(1:22)])
  TAXIOUT CANCELLED CANCELLATIONCODE DIVERTED
1      NA         0             <NA>        0
2      NA         0             <NA>        0
3      NA         0             <NA>        0
4      NA         0             <NA>        0
5      NA         0             <NA>        0
6      NA         0             <NA>        0R> #Row selection
R> df1 <- df[df$DEST=="SFO",]
R> class(df1)
[1] "ore.frame"
attr(,"package")
[1] "OREbase"
R> df2 <- df[df$DEST=="SFO",c(1,3)]
R> df3 <- df[df$DEST=="SFO" | df$DEST=="BOS",1:3]
R> head(df1)
  YEAR DEST ARRDELAY
1 1987  SFO       24
2 1987  SFO       68
3 1987  SFO       -3
4 1987  SFO        5
5 1987  SFO       37
6 1987  SFO       11
R> head(df2)
  YEAR ARRDELAY
1 1987       24
2 1987       68
3 1987       -3
4 1987        5
5 1987       37
6 1987       11
R> head(df3)
  YEAR DEST ARRDELAY
1 1987  SFO       24
2 1987  SFO       68
3 1987  SFO       -3
4 1987  SFO        5
5 1987  SFO       37
6 1987  BOS       NA
```

For joining data, R provides the function merge. In ORE, merge is overridden to work on ore.frame objects. In Example 3, two data frames are created and then merged. Taking the same data, database tables are created using ore.create to enable repeating the invocation using ore.frame objects representing database tables. The results are the same between the two merge invocations, as shown in Listing 2.

Example 3:

```
df1 <- data.frame(x1=1:5, y1=letters[1:5])
df2 <- data.frame(x2=5:1, y2=letters[11:15])
merge (df1, df2, by.x="x1", by.y="x2")


ore.drop(table="TEST_DF1")
ore.drop(table="TEST_DF2")


ore.create(df1, table="TEST_DF1")
ore.create(df2, table="TEST_DF2")
merge (TEST_DF1, TEST_DF2,
       by.x="x1", by.y="x2")
```

Listing 2   *Merge results*

```
R> df1 <- data.frame(x1=1:5, y1=letters[1:5])
R> df2 <- data.frame(x2=5:1, y2=letters[11:15])
R> merge (df1, df2, by.x="x1", by.y="x2")
  x1 y1 y2
1  1  a  o
2  2  b  n
3  3  c  m
4  4  d  l
5  5  e  k
R>
R> ore.drop(table="TEST_DF1")
R> ore.drop(table="TEST_DF2")
R>
R> ore.create(df1, table="TEST_DF1")
R> ore.create(df2, table="TEST_DF2")
R> merge (TEST_DF1, TEST_DF2,
+        by.x="x1", by.y="x2")
  x1 y1 y2
1  5  e  k
2  4  d  l
3  3  c  m
4  2  b  n
5  1  a  o
```

The R documentation for merge notes an all argument that if set to FALSE gives a natural join—a special case of inner join. Another argument, all.x = TRUE, gives a left (outer) join, all.y = TRUE produces a right (outer) join, and all=TRUE produces a (full) outer join. The same arguments apply in ORE.

The function merge can take an argument incomparables that identifies values that cannot be matched. Often, this is set to NA for the missing value. RDBMSs do not match NULLs when doing comparison, which would be the equivalent of specifying incomparables = NA in R. Such functionality requires special handling, for example, to convert the missing values to some other value first.

To transform data, for example, recoding, Example 4 depicts using the transform function. Each transformation is listed as an argument to the transform function, with an ore.frame object as the first argument. The ifelse function performs the recoding and assigns the result to the named columns.

Example 4:

```
ONTIME_S <- transform(ONTIME_S,
        DIVERTED = ifelse(DIVERTED == 0, 'Not Diverted',
                    ifelse(DIVERTED == 1, 'Diverted', '')),
        CANCELLATIONCODE =
                    ifelse(CANCELLATIONCODE == 'A', 'A CODE',
                    ifelse(CANCELLATIONCODE == 'B', 'B CODE',
                    ifelse(CANCELLATIONCODE == 'C', 'C CODE',
                    ifelse(CANCELLATIONCODE == 'D', 'D CODE', 'NOT CANCELLED')))),
        ARRDELAY = ifelse(ARRDELAY > 200, 'LARGE',
                    ifelse(ARRDELAY >= 30, 'MEDIUM', 'SMALL')),
        DEPDELAY = ifelse(DEPDELAY > 200, 'LARGE',
                    ifelse(DEPDELAY >= 30, 'MEDIUM', 'SMALL')),
        DISTANCE_ZSCORE =
                    (DISTANCE - mean(DISTANCE, na.rm=TRUE))/sd(DISTANCE, na.rm=TRUE))
```

Persisting R and ORE Objects

The designers of R incorporated the ability to save and load R objects to and from disk. The whole R workspace of objects can be saved to a file, which can be reloaded in a new R session. This allows users to come back to their previous R environment after quitting the R engine. Using this capability, predictive models can be built in one session and saved for scoring in another, or multiple, possibly parallel, R sessions in the future. This is accomplished through the R save and load functions, where one or more objects are serialized and unserialized, respectively. Consider Example 5 where two R objects, a linear model and data.frame, are saved to a file, and then reloaded. When objects are restored, they have the same names as when they were saved.

Example 5:

```
# R Session 1
x1 <- lm(...)
x2 <- data.frame(...)
save(x1,x2,file="myRObjects.RData")

# R Session 2
load("myRObjects.RData")
ls()
"x1"     "x2"
```

One concern for enterprise deployments using this approach is the need to manage such files through the OS file system. File system location information, along with backup, recovery, and security issues, must be factored into the deployed solution. A more database-centric solution is preferred.

In addition, serializing ORE objects, such as ore.frames, and saving them using R save and load does not work across sessions, since any referenced temporary tables or views are not saved across R sessions. If these proxy object references are not saved properly, restoring such objects makes them incomplete and inoperative.

To address this need for saving R and ORE objects in a database-centric manner, ORE provides object persistence in Oracle Database through an *R datastore*. This capability also facilitates passing sets of potentially complex objects to Embedded R Execution functions, either as a named datastore provided as an embedded R function argument, or a statically named datastore within the function. Objects created in one R session can be saved in a single datastore entry in the database. The name of this datastore can be passed to embedded R functions as an argument for loading within that function. Datastore facilitates passing one or multiple objects.

Example 6 is similar to Example 5. The main difference is the use of ore.save and ore.load, and providing the name of the datastore by which to retrieve ORE objects from the database.

Example 6:

```
# R Session 1
x1 <- ore.lm(...)
x2 <- ore.frame(...)
ore.save(x1,x2,name="ds1")

# R Session 2
ore.load(name="ds1")
ls()
"x1"     "x2"
```

In Example 7, a temporary `ore.frame`, `DAT1`, is created using `ore.push` on the R data set `iris`. An `ore.lm` model is then built that uses `DAT1`, a standard R `lm` model using the `mtcars` data set, followed by an Oracle Data Mining (ODM) Naïve Bayes model using `ONTIME_S`. Invoking `ore.save` on the three models with the datastore name `"myModels"` stores these objects in the database. Any referenced tables, views, or ODM models remain persistent in the database. When an ORE session ends, ORE objects are treated as temporary database objects and dropped unless explicitly saved in a datastore.

Example 7:

```
DAT1           <- ore.push(iris)
ore.lm.mod     <- ore.lm(Sepal.Length ~ ., DAT1 )
lm.mod         <- lm(mpg ~ cyl + disp + hp + wt + gear, mtcars)
nb.mod         <- ore.odmNB(YEAR ~ ARRDELAY + DEPDELAY + log(DISTANCE), ONTIME_S)
ore.save(ore.lm.mod, lm.mod, nb.mod, name = "myModels", overwrite=TRUE)
ore.datastore("myModels")
```

The function `ore.save` has several optional arguments, for example, users may provide the names of specific objects, or provide a list of objects. Users can also specify a particular environment to search for the objects to save. The argument `overwrite`, if set to TRUE, will overwrite an existing named datastore. If `append` is set to TRUE, objects can be added to an existing datastore. Users may also provide descriptive text for the datastore that appears in a summary listing. To view the contents of a datastore, the function `ore.datastoreSummary`, which takes the datastore name as argument, lists each object's name, class, size, and length. If the object is a `data.frame` or `ore.frame`, the number of rows and columns are also provided.

The `ore.load` function restores the saved R objects to the `.GlobalEnv` environment by default. Consider the case where a new R engine is started and connected to the database schema just used to save these objects. After invoking `ore.load` with the name `"myModels,"` the saved objects can be referenced by their original names. Function `ore.load` has the flexibility to load all objects from the datastore, or a list of named objects within the datastore. Users can also specify the environment into which these objects should be loaded if different from `.GlobalEnv`.

In the section "Embedded R Execution," the use of datastores is revisited with the SQL API.

Data Preparation for Time Series

Time series data exists in many domains. Stock and trading data and retail and employment data are just a few examples. The ability to filter, order, and transform time series data often is a prerequisite for understanding trends and seasonal effects.

R has a rich set of time series analysis packages that can take advantage of data preprocessing using ORE filtering, aggregation, and moving window functions on large time series data. See the *CRAN Task View for Time Series Analysis* for a complete list. While ORE leverages R time series functions to perform, for example, forecasting using an ARIMA model, until that final step, the data preparation can be pushed to the database for execution.

ORE provides support for analyzing time series data through date and time transparency, by mapping Oracle date-related data types, such as DATE and TIMESTAMP, to R data types. Through the Transparency Layer, R users can perform date arithmetic, aggregations and percentiles, as well as moving window calculations, such as rolling max and rolling mean, among others.

In Oracle Database, the representations for date and time are unified—there is a single concept to capture this. However, R uses several classes and representations for date and time data, for example, `Date`, `POSIXct`, `POSIXlt`, and `difftime`. Including date and time processing in ORE enables providing a consistent mapping between data types for transparent database data access.

Table 4 lists the mapping of SQL data types to ORE data types for date and time. Notice that ORE introduces `ore.datetime` and `ore.difftime` as new data types. For `INTERVAL YEAR TO MONTH`, `ore.character` is a primitive type, so SQL `INTERVAL YEAR TO MONTH` columns are converted to character strings. While users can work with tables containing these columns, such columns will be treated as simple strings.

As part of the Transparency Layer, users can perform a wide range of operations on date and time data, ranging from binary operations, row functions, vector operations, aggregates, set operations, group by analysis, and moving window aggregation. The function `ore.sort` can be used with date and time columns, as well as `ore.groupApply`'s INDEX argument in Embedded R Execution.

Example 8 illustrates some of the statistical aggregate functions. For data, a sequence of 500 dates spread evenly throughout 2001 is generated along with a random `difftime` and a vector of random normal values. This `data.frame` is pushed to Oracle Database using `ore.push`, which creates an `ore.frame` corresponding to a temporary database table.

Oracle SQL Data Type	ORE Data Type
DATE	ore.datetime
TIMESTAMP	ore.datetime
TIMESTAMP WITH TIME ZONE	ore.datetime
TIMESTAMP WITH LOCAL TIME ZONE	ore.datetime
INTERVAL YEAR TO MONTH	ore.character
INTERVAL DAY TO SECOND	ore.difftime

TABLE 4. *Oracle SQL Date-Related Data Types Mapping to ORE Data Types*

Example 8:

```
N <- 500
mydata <- data.frame(datetime =
            seq(as.POSIXct("2001/01/01"), as.POSIXct("2001/12/31"),
                length.out = N),
            difftime = as.difftime(runif(N), units = "mins"),
            x = rnorm(N))
MYDATA <- ore.push(mydata)
class(MYDATA)
class(MYDATA$datetime)
head(MYDATA,3)
## statistic aggregates
min(MYDATA$datetime)
max(MYDATA$datetime)
range(MYDATA$datetime)
median(MYDATA$datetime)
quantile(MYDATA$datetime, probs = c(0, 0.05, 0.10))
```

The statistical aggregates of min, max, range, median, and quantile produce results on the ore.frame and are computed in the database. Notice that MYDATA is an ore.frame and the datetime column is of class ore.datetime, as shown in Listing 3. For example, the minimum date value is January 1, 2001. Using the quantile function, produce results for the 0, 5 percent, and 10 percent quantiles. Consider computing this on a table with millions or billions of entries. To perform this in R would require loading the full data set to the client, if that were even possible due to memory constraints. With ORE, this is done transparently in the database.

Listing 3 *Results for statistical aggregates involving dates*

```
R> class(MYDATA)
[1] "ore.frame"
attr(,"package")
[1] "OREbase"
R> class(MYDATA$datetime)
[1] "ore.datetime"
attr(,"package")
[1] "OREbase"
R> head(MYDATA,3)
             datetime        difftime          x
1 2001-01-01 00:00:00 54.459730 secs 1.5160605
2 2001-01-01 17:30:25 25.298211 secs 1.0586786
3 2001-01-02 11:00:50  1.654283 secs 0.9161595
R> ## statistic aggregates
R> min(MYDATA$datetime)
[1] "2001-01-01 EST"
R> max(MYDATA$datetime)
```

```
[1] "2001-12-31 EST"
R> range(MYDATA$datetime)
[1] "2001-01-01 EST" "2001-12-31 EST"
R> median(MYDATA$datetime)
[1] "2001-07-02 01:00:00 EDT"
R> quantile(MYDATA$datetime, probs = c(0, 0.05, 0.10))
                          0%                      5%                     10%
  "2001-01-01 00:00:00 EST" "2001-01-19 04:48:00 EST" "2001-02-06 09:36:00 EST"
```

Sampling

Sampling is an important capability for statistical analytics. To perform sampling in R, users must either load the data fully into memory or, if the data is too large to load into R at once, load subsets of the data and construct a sample from each subset. With ORE, instead of pulling the data and then sampling, users can sample directly in the database and either pull only those records that are part of the sample into R, or leave the sample as an `ore.frame` in the database for further processing.

ORE enables a wide range of sampling techniques, for example:

- Simple random sampling

- Split data sampling

- Systematic sampling

- Stratified sampling

- Cluster sampling

- Quota sampling

- Accidental/convenience sampling

    - Via row order access

    - Via hashing

Consider Example 9 for simple random sampling, which involves selecting rows at random. A small demo `data.frame` is created and pushed to the database, creating an `ore.frame`. Out of 20 rows, sample 5 rows using the R `sample` function to produce a random set of indices. This allows getting a sample from `MYDATA`, which is an `ore.frame`, as shown in Listing 4.

Example 9:

```
set.seed(1)
N <- 20
myData <- data.frame(a=1:N,b=letters[1:N])
MYDATA <- ore.push(myData)
```

```
head(MYDATA)
sampleSize <- 5
simpleRandomSample <- MYDATA[sample(nrow(MYDATA), sampleSize), , drop=FALSE]
class(simpleRandomSample)
simpleRandomSample
```

Listing 4   *Simple random sampling results*

```
R> set.seed(1)
R> N <- 20
R> myData <- data.frame(a=1:N,b=letters[1:N])
R> MYDATA <- ore.push(myData)
R> head(MYDATA)
  a b
1 1 a
2 2 b
3 3 c
4 4 d
5 5 e
6 6 f
R> sampleSize <- 5
R> simpleRandomSample <- MYDATA[sample(nrow(MYDATA), sampleSize), , drop=FALSE]
R> class(simpleRandomSample)
[1] "ore.frame"
attr(,"package")
[1] "OREbase"
R> simpleRandomSample
     a b
4    4 d
6    6 f
8    8 h
11 11 k
16 16 p
```

Embedded R Execution

Embedded R Execution refers to the ability to execute R code on the database server, where one or more R engines are dynamically started, controlled, and managed by Oracle Database. By having the R engine on the database server machine, the need to pull data into the user's client R engine is eliminated. Moreover, data transfer is more efficient between the database-side R engine and Oracle Database. Embedded R Execution also enables data-parallel and task-parallel execution of R functions.

While ORE provides an R interface to enable interactive execution of embedded R functions, the SQL interface enables database applications to invoke R scripts seamlessly as part of SQL statements, supporting database-based applications. In addition, results from R functions can be returned as standard database tables for structured data or rich XML with both structured data and complex R objects.

Embedded R Execution also enables returning PNG images produced by R graphics functions. These can be returned in a table with a BLOB column containing the PNG image representation, or as an XML string containing the base 64 encoding of the PNG image. Since R provides a rich environment for producing high-quality and sophisticated graphics, applications can generate such images at the database server and feed these to OBIEE dashboards, reports with BI Publisher, or similar tools.

Embedded R Execution allows users to work with CRAN packages on the database server. Desired packages are installed in the database server R engine and loaded in the R function being executed (via `library(<package>)`), just as they would if executed at the client. It should be noted that ORE does not modify CRAN packages to take advantage of the Transparency Layer's in-database execution, nor does it automate parallel or scalable execution of CRAN packages. The original package behavior and characteristics for scalability or performance remain.

Embedded R Execution provides in-database storage and management for the R functions. This *R script repository* can greatly simplify application deployment. R functions can be stored and removed from the R script repository using either the R or SQL API. Viewing R scripts is achieved by accessing the database table `sys.rq_scripts`. An added benefit of the Embedded R Execution SQL API is the ability to schedule R scripts for execution as part of DBMS_SCHEDULER jobs.

It is important to facilitate the use of R script results by applications both during interactive development and testing by data scientists and application developers, and during deployment to streamline inclusion with dashboards and reporting frameworks. As suggested a moment ago, Embedded R Execution yields improved performance and throughput. Since the database server, such as Exadata, is more powerful than a desktop machine, R functions can benefit from significantly greater compute and memory resources.

R Interface

The R interface of Embedded R Execution consists of the functions: `ore.doEval`, `ore.tableApply`, `ore.rowApply`, `ore.groupApply`, and `ore.indexApply`, as shown in Table 5. Each takes an R function, or closure, as one of its arguments, which is the function to invoke at the database server and referred to as *f* in the text that follows. Alternatively, the name of a function stored in the R script repository can be specified. The Embedded R Execution functions provide capabilities intended for different situations.

- `ore.doEval` invokes *f* in the database. There is no automatic loading of `ore.frame` data to *f*, but *f* can be invoked with arguments. `ore.doEval` can return an `ore.frame` object or a serialized R object.

- `ore.tableApply` takes an `ore.frame` as input that is provided all at once to *f*. Like `ore.doEval`, it can return an `ore.frame` object or serialized R objects. Note that care should be taken to ensure the database server R engine can realistically handle the volume of data contained in the table corresponding to the `ore.frame`.

R Interface Function	Purpose and Signature
`ore.doEval()`	Invoke standalone R script supplying function FUN or function name FUN.NAME `ore.doEval(FUN, ..., FUN.VALUE = NULL, FUN.NAME = NULL)`
`ore.tableApply()`	Invoke R script with `ore.frame` as input X `ore.tableApply(X, FUN, ..., FUN.VALUE = NULL, FUN.NAME = NULL, parallel = FALSE)`
`ore.rowApply()`	Invoke R script on one row at a time, or multiple rows in chunks from `ore.frame` X `ore.rowApply(X, FUN, ..., FUN.VALUE = NULL, FUN.NAME = NULL, rows = 1, parallel = FALSE)`
`ore.groupApply()`	Invoke R script on data partitioned by grouping column INDEX of an `ore.frame` X `ore.groupApply(X, INDEX, FUN, ..., FUN.VALUE = NULL, FUN.NAME = NULL, parallel = FALSE)`
`ore.indexApply()`	Invoke R script N times `ore.indexApply(times, FUN, ..., FUN.VALUE = NULL, FUN.NAME = NULL, parallel = FALSE)`
`ore.scriptCreate()`	Create an R script in the database `ore.scriptCreate(name)`
`ore.scriptDrop()`	Drop an R script in the database `ore.scriptDrop(name, FUN)`

TABLE 5.   *ORE Embedded R Execution R Interface Functions*

- `ore.rowApply` allows specifying the number of rows each invocation of *f* should receive. The function *f* is invoked multiple times, potentially in parallel, until all input data is processed. The return value is a list with the return value from each invocation of *f*.

- `ore.groupApply` partitions the input data according to a specified column's values, and invokes *f* on each partition. The return value from `ore.groupApply` is a list containing the return value from each invocation of *f*.

- ore.indexApply invokes *f* N times. The return value is a list with the return value from each invocation of *f*.

- ore.scriptCreate creates an entry in the R script repository for the function *f* with the provided name. Such functions can be referenced by Embedded R Execution functions.

- ore.scriptDrop removes the named function from the R script repository.

For security, since the ability to define R scripts in the database is a powerful capability, only users who are granted the RQADMIN role are allowed to execute the ore.scriptCreate and ore.scriptDrop functions.

The functions ore.tableApply, ore.rowApply, and ore.groupApply each take an ore.frame as input. Functions ore.doEval and ore.indexApply can obtain data differently: They can take no input data, generate their data within the R function, load data from a file, explicitly pull it from the database, or leverage the Transparency Layer. Functions ore.tableApply, ore.rowApply, and ore.groupApply can access data similarly to supplement the data passed as a function argument.

The return value of the R function, specified using FUN.VALUE, can either be null, which results in an ore.object being returned, or a data.frame signature, which results in an ore.frame being returned from the function.

Embedded R Execution functions can take a variable number of arguments, corresponding to those of the function *f*. Arguments are passed to the function on invocation using the same name as specified in the defined R function. There are special *control arguments* with reserved names that affect the behavior of Embedded R Execution. For example, ore.connect set to TRUE enables auto-connection. This and other control arguments are discussed in more detail later.

Row apply allows specifying the number of rows to process as one chunk. This is valuable to perform batch scoring in parallel since multiple R engines can be leveraged. Group apply allows specifying the column on which to partition data, which also enables parallel execution.

Each Embedded R Execution function requires the specification of the R function to execute, either as a string that contains the R function (using the FUN argument), or the name of an R script that has already been created in the R script repository (using the FUN.NAME argument).

To illustrate using Embedded R Execution, consider the simple R script shown in Example 10 and illustrated in Figure 8. It illustrates getting a structured result back from the R function, such as a data.frame. Since data is generated within the function, this script uses ore.doEval. The function argument scales the first n integers by the argument scale. Notice that argument values num=10 and scale =100 are provided as defaults to the R function.

Example 10:

```
res <-
    ore.doEval(function (num = 10, scale = 100) {
            ID <- seq(num)
            data.frame(ID = ID, RES = ID / scale)
            })
class(res)
res
local_res <- ore.pull(res)
class(local_res)
local_res
```

The R script is passed through the client R engine to the database. The database spawns an R engine on the database server to execute the embedded R function. The result is passed back to the database, and then to the client R engine. The result `res` is returned as a serialized `ore.object`. When printed, this object is deserialized as an R `data.frame`. If the result is pulled to the client using `ore.pull`, it is materialized as a `data.frame`.

Note how seamlessly these embedded R functions blend with the rest of the R code. User-defined R functions can be passed any R object as input created in the R session, and the output can be pulled to the client, if desired. The results are shown in Listing 5.

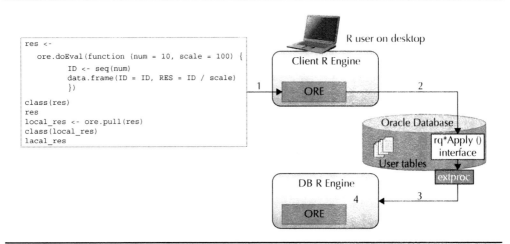

FIGURE 8. *Example using ORE Embedded R Execution with* `ore.doEval`

Listing 5   *Results for ORE Embedded R Execution Example 10*

```
R> res <-
+     ore.doEval(function (num = 10, scale = 100) {
+             ID <- seq(num)
+             data.frame(ID = ID, RES = ID / scale)
+             })
R> class(res)
[1] "ore.object"
attr(,"package")
[1] "OREbase"
R> res
   ID  RES
1   1 0.01
2   2 0.02
3   3 0.03
4   4 0.04
5   5 0.05
6   6 0.06
7   7 0.07
8   8 0.08
9   9 0.09
10 10 0.10
R> local_res <- ore.pull(res)
R> class(local_res)
[1] "data.frame"
R> local_res
   ID  RES
1   1 0.01
2   2 0.02
3   3 0.03
4   4 0.04
5   5 0.05
6   6 0.06
7   7 0.07
8   8 0.08
9   9 0.09
10 10 0.10
```

In Example 11, the arguments for num and scale are passed to the function. These appear as additional arguments to the ore.doEval function. Recall that in the ore.doEval function signature, these are represented as "...". The names of these arguments are the same as those in the R function definition.

Example 11:

```
res <-
    ore.doEval(function (num = 10, scale = 100) {
                ID <- seq(num)
                data.frame(ID = ID, RES = ID / scale)
                },
            num = 20, scale = 1000)
class(res)
res
```

In Example 12, a named script "SimpleScript1" is created in the R script repository and invoked using ore.doEval with the argument FUN.NAME, which is the function name in the repository. The ability to store R scripts in the database and reference them by name is a major convenience when writing database applications that use results from R.

Example 12:

```
ore.scriptDrop("SimpleScript1")
ore.scriptCreate("SimpleScript1",
            function (num = 10, scale = 100) {
                ID <- seq(num)
                data.frame(ID = ID, RES = ID / scale)
                })
res <- ore.doEval(FUN.NAME="SimpleScript1",
                    num = 20, scale = 1000)
```

Example 13 illustrates data parallel execution through the database using the function ore.groupApply. The user-defined R function specifies to build a linear model predicting airline flight arrival delay. However, the goal is to build one model per destination airport. This is specified using the INDEX argument in ore.groupApply. When ore.groupApply is finished executing, an ore.list proxy object is returned. The actual result remains in the database. The ore.list object can be involved in subsequent operations or retrieved to the client R engine for local operations.

Example 13:

```
modList <- ore.groupApply(
    X=ONTIME_S,
    INDEX=ONTIME_S$DEST,
```

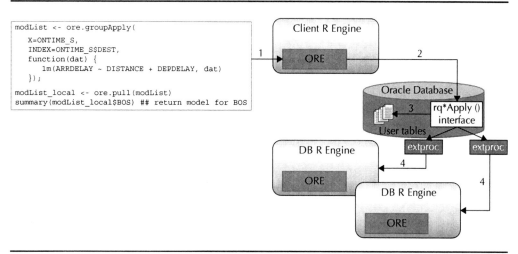

```
modList <- ore.groupApply(
   X=ONTIME_S,
   INDEX=ONTIME_S$DEST,
   function(dat) {
      lm(ARRDELAY ~ DISTANCE + DEPDELAY, dat)
   });

modList_local <- ore.pull(modList)
summary(modList_local$BOS) ## return model for BOS
```

FIGURE 9.   *Example using ORE Embedded R Execution with* `ore.groupApply`

```
function(dat) {
    lm(ARRDELAY ~ DISTANCE + DEPDELAY, dat)
  });
modList_local <- ore.pull(modList)
summary(modList_local$BOS) ## return model for BOS
```

So what is happening behind the scenes? Through `ore.groupApply`, the embedded R function (the one that builds the model using `lm`) is sent to the database, as depicted in Figure 9. The data is partitioned by the `INDEX` column, `DEST`. Next, the database server `rq*Apply` interface starts external process R engines—one per data partition—and loads the data efficiently into the `dat` argument of the function. The resulting models are returned as a single `ore.list` object to the R client, with one model per destination airport. As with `ore.rowApply`, potentially many database server-side R engines can be spawned (or reused) to get *painless* data parallelism, managed by the database. The number of R engines spawned is determined by database *degree of parallelism* settings.

Using the R interface of Embedded R Execution, functions can return not only structured data, but images as well. Example 14a depicts using the Random Forest algorithm to build a model to predict `Species` from the `iris` data set. The defined function produces a `randomForest` model, the model importance, and multidimensional scaling of proximity. It also produces a pairs plot of the predictors. The return value is a `list` of the importance and multidimensional scaling goodness of fit, or GOF.

Example 14a:

```
ore.doEval(function (){
   library(randomForest)
   set.seed(71)
   iris.rf <- randomForest(Species ~ ., data=iris,
                            importance=TRUE, proximity=TRUE)
   imp <- round(importance(iris.rf), 2)
   iris.mds <- cmdscale(1 - iris.rf$proximity, eig=TRUE)
   op <- par(pty="s")
   pairs(cbind(iris[,1:4], iris.mds$points), cex=0.6, gap=0,
         col=c("red", "black", "gray")[as.numeric(iris$Species)],
         main="Iris Data: Predictors and MDS of Proximity Based on RandomForest")
   par(op)
   list(importance = imp, GOF = iris.mds$GOF)
})
```

Listing 6 shows the results of this function. The code shows the structured result, and the illustration that follows shows the pairs plot returned to the user's desktop R client. Both the structured results and the image were generated by an R engine at the database server.

Listing 6 *Results for ORE Embedded R Execution Example 14a*

```
R> library(randomForest)
R> ore.doEval(function (){
+    library(randomForest)
+    set.seed(71)
+    iris.rf <- randomForest(Species ~ ., data=iris,
+                             importance=TRUE, proximity=TRUE)
+    imp <- round(importance(iris.rf), 2)
+    iris.mds <- cmdscale(1 - iris.rf$proximity, eig=TRUE)
+    op <- par(pty="s")
+    pairs(cbind(iris[,1:4], iris.mds$points), cex=0.6, gap=0,
+          col=c("red", "black", "gray")[as.numeric(iris$Species)],
+          main="Iris Data: Predictors and MDS of Proximity Based on RandomForest")
+          par(op)
+          list(importance = imp, GOF = iris.mds$GOF)
+ })
$importance
             setosa versicolor virginica MeanDecreaseAccuracy MeanDecreaseGini
Sepal.Length   6.04       7.85      7.93                11.51             8.77
Sepal.Width    4.40       1.03      5.44                 5.40             2.19
Petal.Length  21.76      31.33     29.64                32.94            42.54
Petal.Width   22.84      32.67     31.68                34.50            45.77

$GOF
[1] 0.7282700 0.7903363
```

Iris Data: Predictors and MDS of Proximity Based on RandomForest

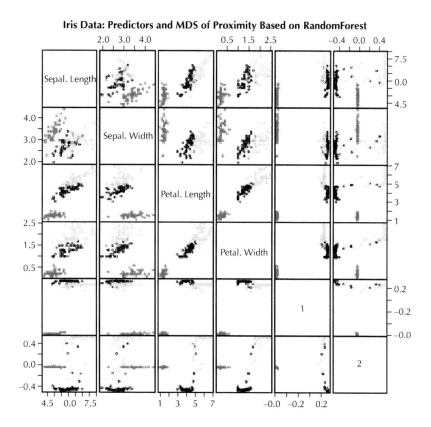

When dealing with PNG images, additional control arguments are available that affect image settings. For example, as shown in Example 14b, including arguments `ore.graphics=TRUE` along with `ore.png.height=700` and `ore.png.width=500`, users can change the aspect ratio of the image. Any arguments allowed by the PNG graphics device driver can be supplied using `ore.png.` as a prefix to arguments of the `png` function.

Example 14b:

```
ore.doEval(function () {
    ...
}, ore.graphics=TRUE, ore.png.height=700, ore.png.width=500)
```

Control arguments in general have the `ore.` prefix. Such arguments are not passed to the user-defined R function, but they control what happens either before or after execution of the R function. Arguments for `ore.connect`, `ore.graphics`, and `ore.png` have been covered already. The argument `ore.drop` controls the input data. If TRUE, a one-column input `data.frame` will be converted to a vector. This input remains as a `data.frame` if set to FALSE.

SQL Interface

The SQL interface consists principally of the functions `rqEval`, `rqTableEval`, `rqRowEval`, and "`rqGroupEval`." (There is not an actual function named `rqGroupEval`, since it needs to be constructed differently in SQL.) In addition, there are two functions, `sys.rqScriptCreate` and `sys.rqScriptDrop`, for managing R scripts—just in the R interface. (See Table 6.)

Recall that one motivation for providing the SQL interface is to allow using ORE within a SQL-based application. Each of these rq*Eval functions provides capabilities intended for different situations. There are similarities to the corresponding R interface functions, but there are important differences too.

Syntactically, the general form consists of a few basic arguments:

```
rq*Eval(
    cursor(select * from <table-1>),
    cursor(select * from <table-2>),
    <output type> or 'select <column list> from <table-3 or dual>',
    <grouping col-name from table-1> or <num rows>,
    '<R-script-name>')
```

The first argument is the input cursor, which specifies the data to be provided to the R function's first argument. This is used for all but the `rqEval` table function. How the data is prepared depends on the type of rq*Eval table function being invoked, just as in the R interface.

As already noted, `rqEval` takes no input data; it just executes the R function, possibly with arguments. `rqTableEval` supplies the entire table at once to the R

SQL Interface Function	Purpose
`rqEval()`	Invoke standalone R script
`rqTableEval()`	Invoke R script with full table as input
`rqRowEval()`	Invoke R script on one row at a time, or multiple rows in chunks
`"rqGroupEval()"`	Invoke R script on data partitioned by grouping column
`sys.rqScriptCreate`	Create named R script
`sys.rqScriptDrop`	Drop named R script

TABLE 6. *ORE SQL Interface Functions*

function. `rqGroupEval` provides one partition of the data to the R function at a time. And, `rqRowEval` supplies up to N rows to the R function.

Arguments can optionally be passed to the R function through a cursor as the second argument. This can include reading values from a table, or from `dual`, but they must be scalar values, and only a single row may be supplied. If there are no arguments, `NULL` should be specified. As discussed later, the *control arguments* discussed in the R interface are also allowed in the SQL interface. To provide control arguments in the SQL syntax, include a "column" as, for example, `cursor(select 1 ore.connect from dual)`, which indicates that the column `ore.connect` is assigned the value 1 (interpreted as TRUE).

The output type can be specified as `NULL`, a SQL select statement, `'XML'`, or `'PNG'`. If NULL, the result is returned as a serialized BLOB. The SQL select statement describes the table definition representing the form of the data returned in the `data.frame` output from the invoked R function. The XML and PNG options are discussed next.

When using the rqGroupEval-style functionality, the next argument would be the column on which to partition the data. All rows with the same value of the specified column are provided to the R function. When using `rqRowEval`, this argument reflects the number of rows to provide to the R function at one time.

The last argument specifies the name of the R function to execute as stored in the R script repository using `sys.rqScriptCreate`. The input arguments to the R function include data from the input cursor (if applicable), and arguments from the arguments cursor.

Example 15 shows how arguments can be passed to the R function `"Example15"`, which takes three arguments: the input `data.frame`, an argument `levels`, and the argument `filename`. Notice that `"ore.connect"` is also provided as a control argument and, as for the R interface, this is not passed to the R function.

Example 15:

```
begin
  sys.rqScriptDrop('Example15');
  sys.rqScriptCreate("Example15",
 'function(dat,levels, filename) {
    ...
  }');
end;
/

select count(*)
from table(rqTableEval(
  cursor ( select x as "x", y as "y", argument_value as "z"
           from geological_model_grid),
```

```
cursor( select 30 as "levels", '/oracle/image.png' as "filename",
        1 "ore.connect" from dual),
NULL,
'Example15'));
```

Passing arguments using this approach allows only scalar numeric and scalar string arguments. To pass nonscalar R objects, such as models or lists, and so on, users can pass the name of a datastore (a scalar) that can be used to load the objects using ore.load within the R function.

In Example 16, a user-defined R function named 'Example16' that builds a linear model and saves the model in a datastore is defined. This function is invoked through the subsequent SQL query. Using the table function rqTableEval, the input data is passed in the first SQL cursor. This data is passed to the first argument dat of the R function. The R function's remaining input arguments are passed in the second cursor, namely ore.connect and the name of the datastore in which to save the model. The result is specified to be returned as an XML string. The last argument is the name of the function to execute, 'Example16'.

Example 16:

```
begin
  sys.rqScriptDrop('Example16');
  sys.rqScriptCreate('Example16',
 'function(dat,datastore_name) {
   mod <- lm(ARRDELAY ~ DISTANCE + DEPDELAY, dat)
   ore.save(mod,name=datastore_name, overwrite=TRUE)
  }');
end;
/
select *
  from table(rqTableEval(
     cursor(select ARRDELAY, DISTANCE, DEPDELAY from   ontime_s),
     cursor(select 1 as "ore.connect", 'myDatastore' as "datastore_name"
            from dual),
     'XML',
     'Example16' ));

-- Part 2
begin
 sys.rqScriptDrop('Example16s');
 sys.rqScriptCreate('Example16s',
 'function(dat, datastore_name) {
    ore.load(datastore_name)
    prd <- predict(mod, newdata=dat)
    prd[as.integer(rownames(prd))] <- prd
    res <- cbind(dat, PRED = prd)
    res}');
end;
/
```

```
select *
from table(rqTableEval(
    cursor(select ARRDELAY, DISTANCE, DEPDELAY from   ontime_s
           where  year = 2003 and month = 5 and dayofmonth = 2),
    cursor(select 1 as "ore.connect",
                  'myDatastore' as "datastore_name" from dual),
    'select ARRDELAY, DISTANCE, DEPDELAY, 1 PRED from ontime_s',
    'Example16s'))
order by 1, 2, 3;
```

In the second part of Example 16, data is scored using the model. The function named 'Example16s', also stored in the R script repository, first loads the model from the datastore before computing the predictions. In the SQL query, rqTableEval's first argument specifies the data to score. R function arguments are again provided in the second argument. The name of the datastore indicates which R model to load. The return value is specified as a table with four named columns. The results of the execution are provided in Listing 7.

Listing 7 *ORE Embedded R Execution using `rqTableEval` results for Example 16*

```
SQL> begin
  sys.rqScriptDrop('Example16');
  sys.rqScriptCreate('Example16',
 'function(dat,datastore_name) {
   mod <- lm(ARRDELAY ~ DISTANCE + DEPDELAY, dat)
   ore.save(mod,name=datastore_name, overwrite=TRUE)
   }');
end;
/
select *
  from table(rqTableEval(
     cursor(select ARRDELAY, DISTANCE, DEPDELAY from   ontime_s),
     cursor(select 1 as "ore.connect", 'myDatastore' as "datastore_name"
            from dual),
     'XML',
     'Example16' ));
  2    3    4    5    6    7    8    9
PL/SQL procedure successfully completed.

SQL>  2    3    4    5    6    7

NAME
--------------------------
VALUE
--------------------------

<root><ANY_obj><ROW-ANY_obj><value></value></ROW-ANY_obj></ANY_obj></root>

SQL> -- Part 2
begin
 sys.rqScriptDrop('Example16s');
 sys.rqScriptCreate('Example16s',
```

```
'function(dat, datastore_name) {
    ore.load(datastore_name)
    prd <- predict(mod, newdata=dat)
    prd[as.integer(rownames(prd))] <- prd
    res <- cbind(dat, PRED = prd)
    res}');
end;
/
select *
from table(rqTableEval(
    cursor(select ARRDELAY, DISTANCE, DEPDELAY from   ontime_s
           where  year = 2003 and month = 5 and dayofmonth = 2),
    cursor(select 1 as "ore.connect",
                  'myDatastore' as "datastore_name" from dual),
    'select ARRDELAY, DISTANCE, DEPDELAY, 1 PRED from ontime_s',
    'Example16s'))
order by 1, 2, 3;
SQL>   2     3     4     5     6     7     8     9     10    11
PL/SQL procedure successfully completed.

SQL>   2     3     4     5     6     7     8     9

  ARRDELAY    DISTANCE    DEPDELAY         PRED
---------- ---------- ---------- ----------
       -24        1190         -2 -3.1485154
       -20         185         -9 -8.6626137
       -16         697         -9 -9.2859791
       -15         859         -8 -8.5206878
       -15        2300         -4 -6.4250082
       -10         358          0 -.21049053
       -10         719         -8 -8.3502363
        -8         307         -2 -2.0734536
        -4        1050         -5 -5.8656481
        -3         150          5 4.85539194
        -2         140         -5 -4.7577135
...
```

For the output of rq*Eval functions, recall that data can be returned in XML or PNG formats. This is useful in several contexts. Since R script output often does not conform to a predefined table structure and can have heterogeneous data results, rich XML output allows applications embedding ORE to work with complex statistical results, new data, and graphs.

Oracle BI Publisher uses XML to populate documents. This XML can be dynamically generated using the Embedded R Execution SQL interface and fed to BI Publisher, or any other tool or application that can consume XML. By wrapping R objects through this generic and powerful XML framework, operational XML-based applications can readily integrate R executed via SQL.

The PNG output type indicates that PNG image streams should be returned. PNG image streams enable database-based applications to consume images directly from tables. R scripts can produce multiple images. As with XML output, PNG output allows for multiple images, which are returned as multiple rows in a table, with the images stored in a column of type BLOB, for *binary large object*. This feature facilitates direct integration with OBIEE 11.1.1.7 and above through the RPD.

Example 17 is our "Hello World!" example for ORE XML. The R function takes no arguments and returns the string "Hello World!". Its invocation using `rqEval` specifies XML as the output. The results are depicted in Listing 8. Notice the structure of the XML, which includes the value "Hello World!". This technique is what allows loading graphs generated in R into BI Publisher documents, as shown in the next example.

Example 17:

```
set long 20000
set pages 1000
begin
  sys.rqScriptCreate('Example17',
 'function() {"Hello World!"}');
end;
/
select name, value
from table(rqEval(NULL,'XML','Example17'));
```

Listing 8   *ORE Embedded R Execution XML output "Hello World!" results*

```
SQL> set long 20000
set pages 1000
begin
  sys.rqScriptCreate('Example17',
 'function() {"Hello World!"}');
end;
/
select name, value
from table(rqEval(NULL,'XML','Example17'));
SQL> SQL>   2    3    4    5
PL/SQL procedure successfully completed.

SQL>   2
NAME
---------------------------------------------------------------------------
VALUE
---------------------------------------------------------------------------
<root><vector_obj><ROW-vector_obj><value>Hello World!</value></ROW-vector_obj></
vector_obj></root>
```

Example 18 illustrates that ORE has the ability to generate an XML string from a graph produced on the database server, along with structured content. This R script with `rqEval` produces a scatter plot of 100 random normal values. The values 1 to 10 are returned in the variable `res`. Executing this using `rqEval` as before, the XML generated is shown in Listing 9. The resulting graph is captured in Figure 10.

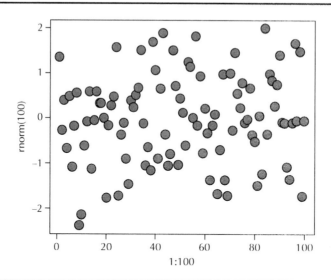

FIGURE 10.   *Scatterplot produced in R function of Example 18*

Example 18:

```
set long 20000
set pages 1000
begin
  sys.rqScriptCreate('Example18',
 'function(){
          res <- 1:10
          plot( 1:100, rnorm(100), pch = 21,
              bg = "red", cex = 2 )
          res
          }');
end;
/
select    value
from      table(rqEval( NULL,'XML','Example18'));
```

Listing 9   *ORE Embedded R Execution XML output with image string results*

```
SQL> set long 20000
set pages 1000
begin
  sys.rqScriptCreate('Example18',
 'function(){
```

```
            res <- 1:10
            plot( 1:100, rnorm(100), pch = 21,
                bg = "red", cex = 2 )
            res
            }');
end;
/
select    value
from      table(rqEval( NULL,'XML','Example18'));
SQL> SQL>  2    3    4    5    6    7    8    9   10
PL/SQL procedure successfully completed.

SQL>   2
VALUE
--------------------------------------------------------------------------------
```

<root><R-data><vector_obj><ROW-vector_obj><value>1</value></ROW-vector_obj><ROW-vector_obj><value>2</value></ROW-vector_obj><ROW-vector_obj><value>3</value></ROW-vector_obj><ROW-vector_obj><value>4</value></ROW-vector_obj><ROW-vector_obj><value>5</value></ROW-vector_obj><ROW-vector_obj><value>6</value></ROW-vector_obj><ROW-vector_obj><value>7</value></ROW-vector_obj><ROW-vector_obj><value>8</value></ROW-vector_obj><ROW-vector_obj><value>9</value></ROW-vector_obj><ROW-vector_obj><value>10</value></ROW-vector_obj></vector_obj></R-data><images><image><img src="data:image/pngbase64"><![CDATA[iVBORw0KGgoAAAANSUhEUgAAAeAAAAHgCAIAAADytinCA
AAgAElEQVR4nOzddVxU2f8/8NfQCAaaiqKwd2K66u0qqMJMHQoSSm2a6LY+kFFF+7C7EVdrdu1AJwURKbFyVbVF
VwbWQXBABEGGRjpnfH/zgOzBzR2IIFfr11OY2KDfZ97aJmmS9AY14Tf15l1hlzPY4IAIIIUQwStECECKjhMKIGKT
EETQoiMogRNCCEyihI0IIBAyEyMNQCyEzhBEZEEoCJEETQoiMogRNCCEyihI0IIBAyEyMNQCyEzhBEZ0OI
IQQIqMoQyi1iyiBE0IITKKEjQhhMgoyMoMNCEEKjKEETQoiMoiMogzhBEZ0II
KIETQghMooSNCGEyChK0IQQIqMoQyi1iyiBE0IITKKEjQhhMoStCEECjK
KIETQghMooSNCGEyChK0IQQIqMoQyi1iyiBE0IITKKEjQhhMgoSNCGEyChI0I
YTIKErQhBAioyhBE0KIjKIETQghMooSNCGEyChK0IQQIqMoQyi1iyiBE0IITKKEjQhhMgoStCECjK
...

Predictive Analytics

The ORE analytics packages consist of OREeda (for exploratory data analysis), OREdm (for data mining), and OREpredict. OREeda contains ORE's database-enabled linear and stepwise regression, and neural network algorithms. OREeda also has Base SAS equivalent functions. OREdm exposes Oracle Data Mining algorithms through an R interface with support for attribute importance, classification, regression, anomaly detection, and clustering. OREpredict provides the function ore.predict, which allows scoring select R models such as rpart and lm in the database—translating the R models to SQL transparently to operate on database data.

OREeda

This subsection provides discussion and examples involving ore.lm, ore.stepwise, and ore.neural.

Functions ore.lm and ore.stepwise   The function ore.lm mimics the R lm least squares regression function, but it performs the calculations on ore.frames, leveraging Oracle Database as the compute engine. It produces the same results as R, but no data is moved from the database to the client to build the model.

The function `ore.stepwise` performs the stepwise least squares regression. With stepwise regression, the choice of predictive variables is performed automatically, by adding terms or removing terms, or both. One objective with stepwise regression is to produce a model with fewer (ideally fewest) terms required for a quality model.

Why provide in-database versions of these popular R algorithms? One motivation is the need to handle data with complex patterns (for example, collinearity) where R does not address the need. The function `ore.stepwise` also provides variable selection criteria used by SAS PROC REG, namely being p-value–based instead of information criteria–based, as is R's `step` function. A side benefit of this is that ORE produces dramatic performance gains. Keeping the data in the database allows building models faster on more data, since the memory limitations of R are avoided.

Table 7 highlights performance results on `ore.stepwise` from the Oracle Micro-Processor Tools environment. On a bilinear model, `ore.stepwise` was 66 times faster than R's `step` function. On a quadratic model, it was 180 times faster.

	Method	R^2	Number of Regressors	mean(rel_error)	Elapsed Time (seconds)
Bilinear model	step	0.9658	86	3.52e–02	2110.0
	ore.stepwise	0.9966	124	3.50e–02	32.1
	Performance difference				ore.stepwise is approximately 65x faster than step at similar R^2 and relative error as stepwise.
Quadratic model	step	0.9962	154	1.05e–02	12600.0
	ore.stepwise	0.9963	210	1.04e–02	69.5
	Performance difference				ore.stepwise is approximately 180x faster than step at similar R^2 relative error.

TABLE 7.   *Performance Results from Oracle Micro-Processor Tools Use of ORE*

The models produced by R's `step` and `ore.stepwise` have a different number of regressors because both the selection mechanisms and interaction terms are handled differently. Function `ore.stepwise` does not differentiate between main terms and interactions, but detects strict linear dependencies and eliminates from the start regressors involved in multicollinear relations. Better performance is a side effect. With `ore.stepwise`, ORE enables the Oracle Micro-Processor Tools environment to significantly expand the data analysis capabilities through R combined with in-database high-performance algorithms, opening the door to new applications.

Let's compare `ore.lm` with R's `lm` function using the `longley` data set. This small macroeconomic data set provides a well-known example for a highly collinear regression and consists of seven economic variables observed yearly over 16 years. The goal is to predict the number of people employed using six predictors such GNP.deflator, GNP, unemployed, and so on. In Listing 10a, the residuals distribution and variable coefficients, among other results, are depicted from the model summary.

Listing 10a   *lm results*

```
R> fit1 <- lm(Employed ~ ., data = longley)
R> summary(fit1)

Call:
lm(formula = Employed ~ ., data = longley)

Residuals:
     Min       1Q    Median       3Q      Max
-0.41011 -0.15767 -0.02816  0.10155  0.45539

Coefficients:
               Estimate Std. Error t value Pr(>|t|)
(Intercept)   -3.482e+03  8.904e+02  -3.911 0.003560 **
GNP.deflator   1.506e-02  8.492e-02   0.177 0.863141
GNP           -3.582e-02  3.349e-02  -1.070 0.312681
Unemployed    -2.020e-02  4.884e-03  -4.136 0.002535 **
Armed.Forces  -1.033e-02  2.143e-03  -4.822 0.000944 ***
Population    -5.110e-02  2.261e-01  -0.226 0.826212
Year           1.829e+00  4.555e-01   4.016 0.003037 **
---
Signif. codes:  0 '***' 0.001 '**' 0.01 '*' 0.05 '.' 0.1 ' ' 1

Residual standard error: 0.3049 on 9 degrees of freedom
Multiple R-squared: 0.9955,     Adjusted R-squared: 0.9925
F-statistic: 330.3 on 6 and 9 DF,  p-value: 4.984e-10
```

To use ore.lm, the function name is changed and an ore.frame is provided. The input ore.frame is created by pushing the longley data.frame to the database using ore.push. Listing 10b depicts that the results are identical.

Listing 10b *ore.lm results*

```
R> LONGLEY <- ore.push(longley)
R> oreFit1 <- ore.lm(Employed ~ ., data = longley)
R> summary(oreFit1)

Call:
ore.lm(formula = Employed ~ ., data = longley)

Residuals:
     Min       1Q    Median       3Q       Max
-0.41011 -0.15980 -0.02816  0.15681   0.45539

Coefficients:
                Estimate Std. Error t value Pr(>|t|)
(Intercept)   -3.482e+03  8.904e+02  -3.911 0.003560 **
GNP.deflator   1.506e-02  8.492e-02   0.177 0.863141
GNP           -3.582e-02  3.349e-02  -1.070 0.312681
Unemployed    -2.020e-02  4.884e-03  -4.136 0.002535 **
Armed.Forces  -1.033e-02  2.143e-03  -4.822 0.000944 ***
Population    -5.110e-02  2.261e-01  -0.226 0.826212
Year           1.829e+00  4.555e-01   4.016 0.003037 **
---
Signif. codes:  0 '***' 0.001 '**' 0.01 '*' 0.05 '.' 0.1 ' ' 1

Residual standard error: 0.3049 on 9 degrees of freedom
Multiple R-squared: 0.9955,     Adjusted R-squared: 0.9925
F-statistic: 330.3 on 6 and 9 DF,  p-value: 4.984e-10
```

Example 19 begins with ore.stepwise, which specifies a formula to consider pairs of variables. Argument add.p as 0.1 is specified, which is the F-test p-value threshold for adding a term to the model. Argument drop.p as 0.1 is also specified, which sets the threshold for removing a term from the model. The ore.stepwise add.p and drop.p arguments behave like SAS PROC REG's SLE and SLS selection criteria, respectively. As shown in Listing 11, the execution results include the summary of steps taken by the algorithm, adding terms with their corresponding residual sum of squares after each model. Notice that because pairs of variables are considered, the variable GNP.deflator is paired with Unemployed in Step 1. The coefficients produced for the selected variables are also provided.

Example 19:

```
LONGLEY <- ore.push(longley)
    # Two stepwise alternatives
oreStep1 <- ore.stepwise(Employed ~ .^2, data = LONGLEY,
                      add.p = 0.1, drop.p = 0.1)
oreStep1
oreStep2 <- step(ore.lm(Employed ~ 1, data = LONGLEY),
              scope = terms(Employed ~ .^2, data = LONGLEY))
oreStep2
```

Listing 11   *Results of executing* `ore.stepwise`

```
R> oreStep1 <- ore.stepwise(Employed ~ .^2, data = LONGLEY,
+                         add.p = 0.1, drop.p = 0.1)
R> oreStep1

Aliased:
[1] "Unemployed:Armed.Forces" "Unemployed:Population"
"Unemployed:Year"
"Armed.Forces:Population"
[5] "Armed.Forces:Year"        "Population:Year"

Steps:
                      Add Drop    RSS Rank
1 GNP.deflator:Unemployed <NA> 384.426    2
2              GNP:Year <NA> 218.957    3
3        GNP.deflator:GNP <NA> 130.525    4
4 GNP.deflator:Population <NA>  81.211    5
5        GNP:Armed.Forces <NA>  18.244    6
6                 Year <NA>  14.492    7

Call:
ore.stepwise(formula = Employed ~ .^2, data = LONGLEY, add.p = 0.1,
    drop.p = 0.1)

Coefficients:
     (Intercept)            Year    GNP.deflator:GNP  GNP.
deflator:Unemployed
GNP.deflator:Population
      -3.539e-01    3.589e-05          -2.978e-03
2.326e-04
        2.303e-05
GNP:Armed.Forces     GNP:Year
        6.875e-06    2.007e-04
```

The second part of Example 19 illustrates building a model using ore.lm, which produces a model that is a subclass of lm. The R step function uses the ore.lm model with the specified scope to iteratively add and drop terms before settling on the "best" model. Here, the scope argument uses terms generated from the provided formula and data. The execution results are shown in Listing 12. Notice how the results of each step are presented. It starts with all the predictors and the effect of dropping each one from the model. It then drops GNP, since that has the lowest AIC value, and continues the process until the model shows no further improvement, that is, the lowest AIC is not better than the AIC shown for the step.

Listing 12   *Results of executing R step with ore.lm*

```
R> oreStep2 <- step(ore.lm(Employed ~ 1, data = LONGLEY),
+                   scope = terms(Employed ~ .^2, data = LONGLEY))
Start:   AIC=41.17
Employed ~ 1

                Df Sum of Sq      RSS     AIC
+ GNP            1    178.973    6.036 -11.597
+ Year           1    174.552   10.457  -2.806
+ GNP.deflator   1    174.397   10.611  -2.571
+ Population      1   170.643   14.366   2.276
+ Unemployed     1     46.716  138.293  38.509
+ Armed.Forces   1     38.691  146.318  39.411
<none>                          185.009  41.165

Step:  AIC=-11.6
Employed ~ GNP

                Df Sum of Sq      RSS     AIC
+ Unemployed     1      2.457    3.579 -17.960
+ Population      1      2.162    3.874 -16.691
+ Year           1      1.125    4.911 -12.898
<none>                           6.036 -11.597
+ GNP.deflator   1      0.212    5.824 -10.169
+ Armed.Forces   1      0.077    5.959  -9.802
- GNP            1    178.973  185.009  41.165

Step:  AIC=-17.96
Employed ~ GNP + Unemployed

                Df Sum of Sq      RSS     AIC
+ Armed.Forces   1      0.822    2.757 -20.137
<none>                           3.579 -17.960
+ Year           1      0.340    3.239 -17.556
+ GNP:Unemployed 1      0.182    3.397 -16.795
```

```
+ Population        1      0.097    3.482 -16.399
+ GNP.deflator      1      0.019    3.560 -16.044
- Unemployed        1      2.457    6.036 -11.597
- GNP               1    134.714  138.293  38.509

Step:  AIC=-20.14
Employed ~ GNP + Unemployed + Armed.Forces
                         Df Sum of Sq    RSS     AIC
+ Year                    1     1.898   0.859 -36.799
+ GNP:Unemployed          1     0.614   2.143 -22.168
+ Population              1     0.390   2.367 -20.578
<none>                                  2.757 -20.137
+ Unemployed:Armed.Forces 1     0.083   2.673 -18.629
+ GNP.deflator            1     0.073   2.684 -18.566
+ GNP:Armed.Forces        1     0.060   2.697 -18.489
- Armed.Forces            1     0.822   3.579 -17.960
- Unemployed              1     3.203   5.959  -9.802
- GNP                     1    78.494  81.250  31.999

Step:  AIC=-36.8
Employed ~ GNP + Unemployed + Armed.Forces + Year

                         Df Sum of Sq    RSS     AIC
<none>                                 0.8587 -36.799
+ Unemployed:Year         1    0.0749 0.7838 -36.259
+ GNP:Unemployed          1    0.0678 0.7909 -36.115
+ Unemployed:Armed.Forces 1    0.0515 0.8072 -35.788
+ GNP:Armed.Forces        1    0.0367 0.8220 -35.498
+ Population              1    0.0193 0.8393 -35.163
+ GNP.deflator            1    0.0175 0.8412 -35.129
+ Armed.Forces:Year       1    0.0136 0.8451 -35.054
+ GNP:Year                1    0.0084 0.8502 -34.957
- GNP                     1    0.4647 1.3234 -31.879
- Year                    1    1.8980 2.7567 -20.137
- Armed.Forces            1    2.3806 3.2393 -17.556
- Unemployed              1    4.0491 4.9077 -10.908
R> oreStep2

Call:
ore.lm(formula = Employed ~ GNP + Unemployed + Armed.Forces +
    Year, data = LONGLEY)

Coefficients:
 (Intercept)         GNP   Unemployed  Armed.Forces       Year
   -3.599e+03   -4.019e-02   -2.088e-02    -1.015e-02  1.887e+00
```

Function `ore.neural` The function `ore.neural` implements a neural network algorithm. Neural networks in some sense mimic the function of neurons in the brain. They are very good at nonlinear statistical modeling, able to learn complex nonlinear relationships between input and output variables. Neural networks have been used to find patterns in data, including those associated with function approximation, classification, data processing, and robotics.

The function `ore.neural` supports a single-layer feed-forward neural network for regression. It supports one hidden layer with a specifiable number of nodes and uses the bipolar sigmoid activation function. The output uses the linear activation function. The algorithm benefits from a state-of-the-art numerical optimization engine that provides robustness, accuracy, and a small number of data reads for improved performance. `ore.neural` achieves performance by reading one hundred thousand rows of data in a block, performing computations on that data, and then discarding the block before proceeding to the next block. In contrast, R's nnet requires the entire data set to fit in memory. Note that although the number of rows is unconstrained, the number of columns is currently limited to one thousand, which is the number of columns permitted in a database table.

Consider Example 20, which uses the p53 Mutants data set. The goal is to model mutant p53 transcriptional activity (active vs. inactive) based on data extracted from biophysical simulations. `ore.neural` was able to complete the computation on the full data, whereas R's nnet did not due to memory constraints. To obtain a comparison of error rates, a subset of nine columns from K9 is used to allow nnet to complete. Column V1 is the target against the remaining eight variables. Specifying a neural network with 20 hidden nodes, the nnet script specifies to generate predictions using the input data and to compute the sum of the error squared, which is done in R memory. Essentially the same specification occurs for `ore.neural`. However, the data is first pushed to the database, the model built, and predictions generated in the database. Notice, however, that the error is also computed using the Transparency Layer, in the database.

Example 20:

```
# nnet example
d <- read.csv('./K9-9.data', header=TRUE)
fit <-nnet(V1 ~., data = d, size=20, linout=TRUE)
p <-predict(fit, newdata=d)
z <- p - d$V1
sum(z^2)

# ore.neural example
d <-read.csv('./K9-9.data', header=TRUE)
dd <- ore.push(d)
fit <- ore.neural(V1 ~., data = dd, hiddenSize=20)
pp <- predict(fit, newdata=dd)
z <- pp - dd$V1
sum(z^2)
```

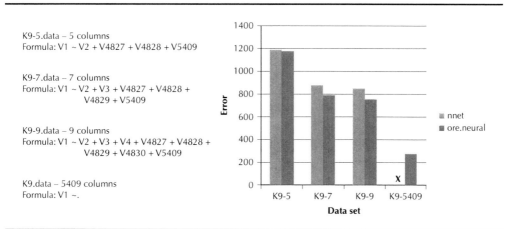

K9-5.data – 5 columns
Formula: V1 ~ V2 + V4827 + V4828 + V5409

K9-7.data – 7 columns
Formula: V1 ~ V2 + V3 + V4827 + V4828 +
            V4829 + V5409

K9-9.data – 9 columns
Formula: V1 ~ V2 + V3 + V4 + V4827 + V4828 +
            V4829 + V4830 + V5409

K9.data – 5409 columns
Formula: V1 ~.

FIGURE 11. *Error rate comparison between* `nnet` *and* `ore.neural`

Figure 11 highlights three things: First, the error rate improves as more predictors are added. Second, `ore.neural` produced lower error rates than `nnet`, consistently. And third, on the full data set, `nnet` did not complete, while `ore.neural` did.

Using the K9 data set, Example 21 builds a neural network model using `ore.neural` with two targets, V1 and V2. A subset of five columns from K9 is pushed to the database, and the model fitted. Notice the use of `cbind` to specify the multiple targets. After scoring the data, the variable `pred` contains a two-column `ore.frame`, one column for each target, or response variable. `cbind` combines the prediction with the original data as depicted in Listing 13. Using `head`, the first two columns contain the predicted values followed by the original target columns and predictors.

Example 21:

```
dd   <- read.csv('~/K9-5.data', header=TRUE)
od   <- ore.push(dd)
fit  <- ore.neural(cbind(V1, V2) ~ V4827 + V4828 + V5409,
                   data = od, hiddenSize=10)
pred <- predict(fit, newdata=od)
res  <- cbind(pred,od)
head(res)
```

Listing 13 *Results of Example 21 using* `ore.neural` *with two targets*

```
R> dd   <- read.csv('~/K9-5.data', header=TRUE)
R> od   <- ore.push(dd)
R> fit  <- ore.neural(cbind(V1, V2) ~ V4827 + V4828 + V5409,
+                 data = od, hiddenSize=10)
R> pred <- predict(fit, newdata=od)
R> res  <- cbind(pred,od)
R> head(res)
            o1           o2     V1      V2 V4827   V4828 V5409
1 -0.18541160 -0.019421025 -0.161 -0.014 0.023  -0.001    -1
2 -0.11777635 -0.002044806 -0.158 -0.002 0.010   0.003    -1
3 -0.15176917 -0.013006371 -0.169 -0.025 0.016   0.003    -1
4 -0.11975969 -0.006174594 -0.183 -0.051 0.010   0.010    -1
5 -0.12313956 -0.002837944 -0.154  0.005 0.011   0.001    -1
6 -0.08733031  0.008628771 -0.150  0.016 0.005   0.003    -1
```

OREdm

Oracle R Enterprise is part of the Oracle Advanced Analytics (OAA) option to Oracle Database Enterprise Edition. OAA consists of both Oracle R Enterprise and Oracle Data Mining, providing complementary functionality. As a result, the predictive analytics capabilities of the OAA option provide the broadest analytical toolset for the enterprise. The choice of tool within OAA should be based on various factors: the technique required, interface preference, data volume, and skill set.

Oracle Data Mining provides a convenient workflow-based GUI as well as a well-integrated SQL API for model building and scoring. ORE provides a programming interface based both on R and SQL, with the ability to invoke R scripts from SQL. In general, in-database techniques should be used to avoid data access latency and achieve high performance and scalability. ORE exposes several Oracle Data Mining algorithms through R functions. These allow R users to benefit from these powerful in-database data mining algorithms.

ORE appeals to traditional statisticians and quantitative analysts who are comfortable writing R code but need to leverage the database as a computational engine. The ability to execute R scripts through SQL means that R scripts developed by analysts can be more immediately operationalized in production SQL-based applications.

The OREdm package works transparently on database data from R using Oracle Data Mining algorithms. The function signature for building models uses an R formula object to specify *target* and *predictors*, or the *response* and *terms* as referred to in R. Objects of type ore.frame are used to provide input data for model building and data scoring. Data scoring is performed using the overloaded predict function.

The names of most model-building arguments have been matched to corresponding R function arguments. Argument default values are explicitly specified as part of the

Algorithm	Main R Function	Mining Type/Function
Minimum Description Length	`ore.odmAI`	Attribute Importance for Classification or Regression
Decision Tree	`ore.odmDT`	Classification
Generalized Linear Models	`ore.odmGLM`	Classification Regression
KMeans	`ore.odmKMeans`	Clustering
Naïve Bayes	`ore.odmNB`	Classification
Support Vector Machine	`ore.odmSVM`	Classification Regression Anomaly Detection

TABLE 8. *OREdm-Supported Algorithms*

function signature. The result of model building is an R object that references the Oracle Data Mining model in the database.

As for objects in R, models are treated as transient objects. When the session ends, objects are automatically cleaned up. OREdm models are treated similarly with the side effect that the corresponding Oracle Data Mining model is also automatically deleted at the end of an ORE session. If a model needs to persist across R sessions, OREdm model objects can be explicitly saved using the datastore function `ore.save`.

Table 8 lists the set of Oracle Data Mining algorithms supported in ORE, their corresponding R function for building the model, and the mining type or function they support. These in-database algorithms enable attribute importance, classification, regression, anomaly detection, and clustering.

As an example, the function signature for the OREdm Naïve Bayes classification algorithm for building models and scoring is provided here. The function `ore.odmNB` supports Oracle Data Mining's auto-data preparation option and the ability to specify class priors. Users can also specify how to treat rows that contain missing values.

```
ore.odmNB(
    formula,                    # formula specifying attributes for model build
    data,                       # ore.frame of the training data set
    auto.data.prep = TRUE,      # Setting to perform automatic data preparation
    class.priors = NULL,        # data.frame containing target class priors
    na.action = na.pass)        # Allows missing values (na.pass), or removes rows
                                #    with missing values (na.omit)
    predict(
```

```
object,                    # Object of type "ore.naiveBayes"
newdata,                   # Data used for scoring
supplemental.cols = NULL,  # Columns to retain in output
type = c("class","raw"),   # "raw" - cond. a-posterior probs for each class
                           # "class" - class with max prob

na.action = na.pass)
```

The `predict` function, which takes an object of type `ore.odmNB`, allows the specification of supplemental columns, that is, those from `newdata` that should be output with the predictions. Users can also specify whether the single predicted class and probability should be returned, the probability associated with each class, or both.

In the annotated example in Listing 14, the `ORE` package is loaded and a connection to the database made. The data set is the `titanic3` data set from the `PASWR` package, which provides data on survival of passengers aboard the Titanic. This data is pushed to the database and prepared by changing the values of column `survived` from 1 and 0, to Yes and No, respectively. This and subsequent transformations are done using the ORE Transparency Layer. The data is sampled into train and test sets for model building and assessing model quality. Priors can also be set when building a Naïve Bayes model by creating a `data.frame` with prior values per class. The model is built using the function `ore.odmNB` with arguments for the formula specifying the target and predictors, the `ore.frame` data, and the class priors `data.frame`.

Listing 14   *Annotated example using `ore.odmNB`*

```
library(ORE) ◄─────── Login to database for transparent access via ORE
ore.connect("rquser","orcl","localhost","rquser",all=TRUE)

data(titanic3,package="PASWR")
t3 <- ore.push(titanic3) ◄────── Push data to db for transparent access
                                        Recode column from 0/1
t3$survived <- ifelse(t3$survived == 1, "Yes", "No") ◄──── to No/Yes keeping data in
n.rows <- nrow(t3)                                          database

set.seed(seed=6218945)
random.sample <- sample(1:n.rows, ceiling(n.rows/2))
t3.train <- t3[random.sample,]
t3.test  <- t3[setdiff(1:n.rows,random.sample),] ◄───────Sample keeping data in database

priors <- data.frame( ◄───────Create priors for model building
    TARGET_VALUE = c("Yes", "No"),
    PRIOR_PROBABILITY = c(0.1, 0.9))

nb  <- ore.odmNB(survived ~ pclass+sex+age+fare+embarked,
            t3.train, class.priors=priors) ◄─────── Build model using R formula
                                                    using Transparency Layer data
nb.res  <- predict (nb, t3.test,"survived") ◄─────── Score data using ore.frame
head(nb.res,10) ◄───── Display first ten rows        with OREdm model object
                       of data frame using
                       Transparency Layer
```

```
with(nb.res, table(survived,PREDICTION, dnn = c("Actual","Predicted")))

library(verification)
res <- ore.pull(nb.res)
perf.auc <- roc.area(ifelse(res$survived == "Yes", 1, 0), res$'Yes')
auc.roc <- signif(perf.auc$A, digits=3)
auc.roc.p <- signif(perf.auc$p.value, digits=3)
roc.plot(ifelse(res$survived == "Yes", 1, 0), res$'Yes', binormal=T, plot="both",
        xlab="False Positive Rate",
        ylab="True Postive Rate", main= "Titanic survival ODM NB model ROC
Curve")
text(0.7, 0.4, labels= paste("AUC ROC:", signif(perf.auc$A, digits=3)))
text(0.7, 0.3, labels= paste("p-value:", signif(perf.auc$p.value, digits=3)))
nb
summary(nb)
ore.disconnect()
```

Compute confusion matrix using Transparency Layer

Retrieve result from database for using verification package

View model object summary

Disconnect from database

Model, train, and test objects are automatically removed when session ends or R objects are removed

Continuing in Listing 14, the data is scored using the `predict` function passing the Naïve Bayes model just created. The supplemental column `survived` is included. After looking at the first few rows of scores, a confusion matrix is computed using the Transparency Layer function `table`. To illustrate using in-database results with open source packages, the `verification` package is loaded and the data pulled to the client R engine. The final steps involve computing and plotting the ROC metric, viewing the model summary, and disconnecting from the database. Upon exiting the R session, or removing the Naïve Bayes object stored in the variable `nb`, the Oracle Data Mining model in the database is automatically deleted. No further cleanup is required.

Listing 15 shows the model summary, followed by the ROC Curve. ROC provides a metric for assessing model quality, and for comparing models. The further the curve is to the upper left, the better the model. A typical additional metric is the AUC, or *area under the curve*, which gives a single value for comparison.

Listing 15 *Results from annotated `ore.odmNB` example*

```
R> summary(nb)

Call:
ore.odmNB(formula = survived ~ pclass + sex + age + fare + embarked,
    data = t3.train, class.priors = priors)

Settings:
          value
prep.auto    on
```

```
Apriori:
 No Yes
0.9 0.1

Tables:
$embarked
     'Cherbourg' 'Queenstown', 'Southampton'
No     0.1569620                  0.8430380
Yes    0.3178295                  0.6821705

$fare
     ( ; 51.931249600000001), [51.931249600000001; 51.931249600000001]
(51.931249600000001;   )
No                                                       0.91370558
0.08629442
Yes                                                      0.67307692
0.32692308

$pclass
     '1st', '2nd'      '3rd'
No     0.3417722 0.6582278
Yes    0.6346154 0.3653846

$sex
       female      male
No   0.1670886 0.8329114
Yes 0.6769231 0.3230769


Levels:
[1] "No"  "Yes"
```

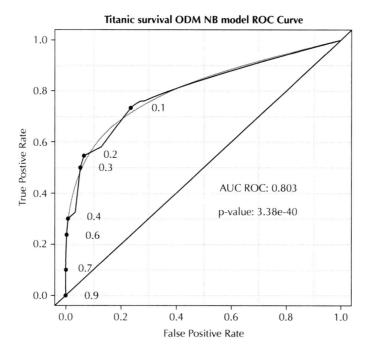

OREpredict

The OREpredict package provides a commercial-grade scoring engine for R-generated models. This means high-performance, scalable, in-database scoring on ore.frames, but using models built via popular R functions. OREpredict also simplifies application workflow, since data need not be pulled to an R engine for scoring. The OREpredict functions generate SQL using the R model details. The main function is ore.predict, which is an S4 generic function, where a specific method exists for each R model type that ORE supports.

Table 9 lists the R models supported in OREpredict.

Example 22 illustrates using the iris data set to first build a linear model using the R lm function to predict Sepal.Length and then predict using OREpredict. The iris data set is pushed to the database and ore.predict is invoked using the irisModel created in R. Note that the ore.frame IRIS (in capitals) is provided as the data to be scored.

Class	Package	Description
glm	`stats`	Generalized Linear Model
negbin	`MASS`	Negative binomial Generalized Linear Model
hclust	`stats`	Hierarchical Clustering
kmeans	`stats`	K-Means Clustering
lm	`stats`	Linear Model
multinom	`nnet`	Multinomial Log-Linear Model
nnet	`nnet`	Neural Network
rpart	`rpart`	Recursive Partitioning and Regression Tree

TABLE 9. *OREpredict-supported R models*

Example 22:

```
irisModel <- lm(Sepal.Length ~ ., data = iris)
IRIS      <- ore.push(iris)
IRISpred  <- ore.predict(irisModel, IRIS, se.fit = TRUE,
                         interval = "prediction")
IRIS <- cbind(IRIS, IRISpred)
head(IRIS)
```

Binding the prediction column to the rest of the data set allows comparison of the prediction with the original sepal length. The results are shown in Listing 16.

Listing 16 *OREpredict results using lm model*

```
R> irisModel <- lm(Sepal.Length ~ ., data = iris)
R> IRIS      <- ore.push(iris)
R> IRISpred  <- ore.predict(irisModel, IRIS, se.fit = TRUE,
+                       interval = "prediction")
R> IRIS <- cbind(IRIS, IRISpred)
R> head(IRIS)
  Sepal.Length Sepal.Width Petal.Length Petal.Width Species    PRED   SE.PRED
LOWER.PRED UPPER.PRED
1          5.1         3.5          1.4         0.2  setosa 5.004788 0.04479188
4.391895   5.617681
2          4.9         3.0          1.4         0.2  setosa 4.756844 0.05514933
4.140660   5.373027
3          4.7         3.2          1.3         0.2  setosa 4.773097 0.04690495
4.159587   5.386607
4          4.6         3.1          1.5         0.2  setosa 4.889357 0.05135928
4.274454   5.504259
5          5.0         3.6          1.4         0.2  setosa 5.054377 0.04736842
```

```
4.440727   5.668026
6          5.4        3.9        1.7        0.4  setosa 5.388886 0.05592364
4.772430   6.005342
```

Summing up predictive analytics, ORE provides a rich set of predictive analytics capabilities that includes in-database algorithms from Oracle Data Mining, ORE-provided algorithms, as well as the ability to supplement existing techniques with those from CRAN. Using select R algorithms, data can be scored directly in the database. In-database model building and scoring yields both performance gains and scalability.

Oracle R Connector for Hadoop

Oracle R Connector for Hadoop (ORCH) provides native R access to a Hadoop cluster, which for Oracle is the Oracle Big Data Appliance. ORCH users can access and manipulate data in HDFS, Oracle Database, and the file system. Further, users can write MapReduce programs exclusively in the R language and invoke MapReduce jobs through a natural R interface. ORCH facilitates transitioning work from the lab to production without requiring knowledge of Hadoop interfaces, the Hadoop call-level interface, or IT infrastructure. This is depicted in Figure 12.

Just as in ORE, where users can leverage CRAN packages at the database server, CRAN packages can also be used to work on HDFS-resident data within mapper and reducer functions. To enable this, such packages must be installed on each task node on the Hadoop cluster.

To introduce programming with ORCH, consider a text analysis example as depicted in Figure 13. The goal is to count the number of times each word occurs in a set of documents, referred to as a *corpus*. In HDFS, these documents are divided

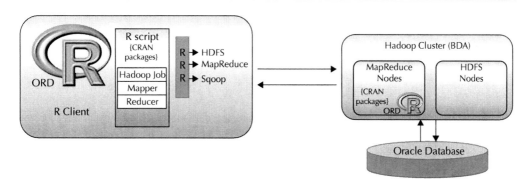

FIGURE 12. *Oracle R Connector for Hadoop Architecture*

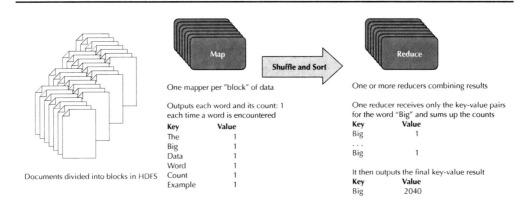

FIGURE 13.   *Text analysis involving word counts using Hadoop*

into blocks and each block is processed by a mapper task. The mapper function parses the text and outputs each word it encounters with the value 1. The text "The Big Data word count example" is output as *key* and *value* pairs, where the key is the word (which may show up multiple times) and the corresponding value is 1. The middle phase, *shuffle and sort*, puts all the values of the same key together and provides them to a reducer. The reducer then sums the values to produce the word count for that particular word.

The corresponding ORCH R code that implements this is provided in Example 23. Data is first loaded from a file and *put* in HDFS using `hdfs.put`. This provides a handle to the HDFS data. The Hadoop job is executed using `hadoop.exec` with this handle, the mapper, reducer, and configuration settings.

Example 23:

```
corpus <- scan("corpus.dat", what=" ",quiet= TRUE, sep="\n")
corpus <- gsub("([/\\\":,#.@-])", " ", corpus)
input  <- hdfs.put(corpus)
res    <- hadoop.exec(dfs.id = input,
            mapper = function(k,v) {
                x <- strsplit(v[[1]], " ")[[1]]
                x <- x[x!='']
                out <- NULL
                for(i in 1:length(x))
                  out <- c(out, orch.keyval(x[i],1))
                out
            },
            reducer = function(k,vv) {
```

```
                    orch.keyval(k, sum(unlist(vv)))
                },
                config = new("mapred.config",
                  job.name       = "wordcount",
                  map.output     = data.frame(key='', val=0),
                  reduce.output  = data.frame(key='', val=0) )
            )
res
hdfs.get(res)
```

The mapper splits the words and outputs each word with the count of 1. This is done using the function `orch.keyval`. The reducer sums the list of values it receives, which is a vector of 1s. The configuration specification allows users to control details of the Hadoop job, for example, a job name to allow identifying a job easily through standard Hadoop tools. More importantly, the format of the mapper and reducer output can be specified. In this example, both the mapper and reducer output specify that the key is a character string and the value is numeric. Lastly, the result is retrieved from HDFS using the function `hdfs.get`.

Invoking MapReduce Jobs

ORCH provides `hadoop.exec` and `hadoop.run` for invoking MapReduce jobs. The function `hadoop.exec` requires input data to reside in HDFS already, whereas `hadoop.run` will attempt to load data such as an `ore.frame` or `data.frame` to HDFS for the user. After the input data, there are four principal sections: *mapper, reducer, variable export,* and *job configuration.* Each mapper receives a set of rows, referred to as a *block,* from HDFS as key-value pairs. The optional *key* has the same data type as that of the input, but the *value* can be either a `list` or `data.frame`. The mapper outputs results to be passed to the reducer using the `orch.keyval` function, which takes two arguments: a key and a value. The value can be any R object if packed with the `orch.pack` function.

Testing ORCH R Scripts Without the Hadoop Cluster

Once a MapReduce job is specified, it is often a good idea to test it locally before unleashing it on the Hadoop cluster, which is likely a shared and valuable resource. To do this, ORCH provides a *dry run* mode where the MapReduce job, and corresponding R code, runs locally, for example, on a laptop or desktop system. This enables testing R code on a sample of the data. To enable a dry run, no change to the MapReduce code is required—simply invoke `orch.dryrun` with the argument value TRUE. Data is obtained from HDFS and streamed into the mapper and reducer functions, which are executed serially on the local machine. As a result, the data likely must be changed to be small enough to fit in memory. Upon job success, the resulting data is placed in HDFS, as it would be if run on the Hadoop cluster.

Example 24 contains a MapReduce job that computes the average arrival delay for all flights to San Francisco. Notice that orch.dryrun is set to TRUE. The mapper checks if the key is "SFO" and then outputs the results. The reducer sums up the arrival delay and takes the average, outputting the key, which is "SFO," and the value, which is the average arrival delay. Finally, the result is output by getting the HDFS file, with the handle stored in res.

Example 24:

```
orch.dryrun(T)
dfs <- hdfs.attach('ontime_R')
res <- NULL
res <- hadoop.run(
    dfs,
    mapper = function(key, ontime) {
        if (key == 'SFO') {
            keyval(key, ontime)
        }
    },
    reducer = function(key, vals) {
        sumAD <- 0
        count <- 0
        for (x in vals) {
            if (!is.na(x$ARRDELAY)) {
                sumAD <- sumAD + x$ARRDELAY
                count <- count + 1
            }
        }
        res <- sumAD / count
        keyval(key, res)
    }
)
res
hdfs.get(res)
```

To have the MapReduce job run on the cluster, simply make one change: set orch.dryrun to FALSE.

```
orch.dryrun(F)
```

The MapReduce code is exactly the same, except perhaps for changing the data from a sample HDFS file to the full data desired.

ORCH also allows the export of any R variable to the mapper and reducer functions. This supports passing data from the client R environment to mapper and reducer functions. The job configuration options allow users to fine-tune how Hadoop operates on the data or interacts with the environment. This is discussed further later.

Interacting with HDFS from R

When working with ORCH, there are a variety of places from which to get data: HDFS, the database, and the file system. For HDFS, as shown in Example 25, ORCH provides functions to obtain the present working directory, list the files in HDFS, make directories, and change directories. On an HDFS file (or more correctly stated, directory), users can ask for its size, the number of component file parts, and get a sample of the data. This sample, however, is not necessarily a random sample. From the database, users can list database tables and perform basic ORE functionality. From R, all the standard functions for interacting with the file system are available.

Example 25:

```
hdfs.pwd()
hdfs.ls()
hdfs.mkdir("xq")
hdfs.cd("xq")
hdfs.ls()
hdfs.size("ontime_s")
hdfs.parts("ontime_s")
hdfs.sample("ontime_s",lines=3)
```

Figure 14 highlights a few examples for getting data into HDFS. Notice that in each case, users can remove an HDFS file using `hdfs.rm`. The first example shows

Data from File
Use hdfs.upload
Key if first column: YEAR
	`hdfs.rm('ontime_File')`
	`ontime.dfs_File <- hdfs.upload('ontime_s2000.dat',`
	`                    dfs.name='ontime_File')`
	`hdfs.exists('ontime_File')`

Data from Database Table
Use hdfs.push
Key column: DEST
	`hdfs.rm('ontime_DB')`
	`ontime.dfs_D <- hdfs.push(ontime_s2000,`
	`                    key='DEST',`
	`                    dfs.name='ontime_DB')`
	`hdfs.exists('ontime_DB')`

Data from R data.frame
Use hdfs.put
Key column: DEST
	`hdfs.rm('ontime_R')`
	`ontime <- ore.pull(ontime_s2000)`
	`ontime.dfs_R <- hdfs.put(ontime,`
	`                    key='DEST',`
	`                    dfs.name='ontime_R')`
	`hdfs.exists('ontime_R')`

FIGURE 14. *Loading data into HDFS using ORCH*

uploading data from the file system to HDFS. The function `hdfs.upload` accepts arguments for the data file and HDFS file name. The first column of the data file is expected to be the key column for the HDFS file. ORCH supports comma-separated-value (CSV) file data.

The second example uses `hdfs.push`, which takes an `ore.frame` as input. The `ore.frame` corresponds to a table in Oracle Database. Data from the database can be pushed to HDFS in a single function call. In addition, the key column can be explicitly specified. In the third example, `hdfs.put` supports loading a `data.frame` into HDFS, also specifying a key column.

Corresponding functions are available to take data from HDFS: `hdfs.get` returns an R in-memory object of the HDFS data, `hdfs.pull` moves data from HDFS to Oracle Database using the underlying Sqoop facility of Hadoop, and `hdfs.download` copies data from HDFS to the local file system.

HDFS Metadata Discovery

ORCH uses metadata about data files stored in a particular HDFS directory to know how to interpret it. ORCH `hdfs.*` functions take HDFS directories as input, not individual files. The filenames within directories can be any valid filename. ORCH requires a valid data directory to include an `__ORCHMETA__` file, which minimally contains the metadata described in Table 10. ORCH allows metadata to be discovered dynamically from CSV files using `hdfs.attach`. However, if files are large, it will be faster to create the ORCHMETA file that describes the HDFS content manually, since data is scanned to determine correct data types.

__ORCHMETA__ Field	Description or Value
orch.kvs	TRUE (the data is key-value type)
orch.names	Column names, for example, "speed," "dist"
orch.class	data.frame
orch.types	Column types, for example, "numeric," "numeric"
orch.dim	Data dimensions (optional), for example, 50,2
orch.keyi	Index of column treated as key 0 means key is null ("\t" character at start of row) –1 means key not available (no tab at start of row)
orch.rownamei	Index of column used for rownames 0 means no rownames

TABLE 10. *__ORCHMETA__ File Structure*

In Figure 15, the upper portion lists the component files in an HDFS directory followed by the content of the metadata file __ORCHMETA__. While the upper portion used the Hadoop command line, the lower portion shows that the same can be done from R using ORCH. The function `hdfs.id` returns a handle to the HDFS file and then `hdfs.describe` allows viewing the metadata content. The metadata describe a `data.frame` with two numeric columns: MOVIE_ID and GENRE_ID, with no key specified. Without a metadata file, users should invoke `hdfs.attach` to auto-discover this metadata.

```
[oracle@bigdatalite 2.13]$ hadoop fs -ls /user/oracle/moviework/advancedanalytics/data/movie_genre_subset
Found 7 items
-rw-r--r--   3 oracle hadoop          0 2012-10-15 12:52 /user/oracle/moviework/advancedanalytics/data/movie_genre_subset/_SUCCESS
-rw-r--r--   3 oracle hadoop        337 2012-10-15 12:52 /user/oracle/moviework/advancedanalytics/data/movie_genre_subset/__ORCHMETA__
drwxr-xr-x   - oracle hadoop          0 2012-10-15 12:51 /user/oracle/moviework/advancedanalytics/data/movie_genre_subset/_logs
-rw-r--r--   3 oracle hadoop      49413 2012-10-15 12:51 /user/oracle/moviework/advancedanalytics/data/movie_genre_subset/part-m-00000
-rw-r--r--   3 oracle hadoop      18038 2012-10-15 12:51 /user/oracle/moviework/advancedanalytics/data/movie_genre_subset/part-m-00001
-rw-r--r--   3 oracle hadoop        671 2012-10-15 12:51 /user/oracle/moviework/advancedanalytics/data/movie_genre_subset/part-m-00002
-rw-r--r--   3 oracle hadoop       4743 2012-10-15 12:52 /user/oracle/moviework/advancedanalytics/data/movie_genre_subset/part-m-00003
[oracle@bigdatalite 2.13]$ hadoop fs -cat /user/oracle/moviework/advancedanalytics/data/movie_genre_subset/__ORCHMETA__
orch.kvs         TRUE
orch.names       "MOVIE_ID","GENRE_ID"
orch.rownamei    0
orch.class       "data.frame"
orch.types       "numeric","numeric"
orch.key1        -1
orch.desc.name   "MOVIE_ID","GENRE_ID"
orch.desc.Sclass         "numeric","numeric"
orch.desc.type   "NUMBER","NUMBER"
orch.desc.len    22,22
orch.desc.precision      0,0
orch.desc.scale -127,-127
orch.desc.nullOK         FALSE,FALSE
```

```
R> mg.dfs <- hdfs.id("/user/oracle/moviework/advancedanalytics/data/movie_genre_subset")
R> mg.dfs
[1] "/user/oracle/moviework/advancedanalytics/data/movie_genre_subset"
attr(,"dfs.id")
[1] TRUE
R> hdfs.describe(mg.dfs)
            name                                                         values
1           path /user/oracle/moviework/advancedanalytics/data/movie_genre_subset
2         origin                                                        unknown
3          class                                                     data.frame
4          types                                               numeric, numeric
5            dim
6          names                                              MOVIE_ID, GENRE_ID
7        has.key                                                          FALSE
8     key.column                                                          -1:NA
9       null.key                                                          FALSE
10   has.rownames                                                         FALSE
11           size                                                          72865
12          parts                                                              4
R> y <- hdfs.attach("/user/oracle/moviework/advancedanalytics/data/movie_genre_subset")
R> y
[1] "/user/oracle/moviework/advancedanalytics/data/movie_genre_subset"
attr(,"dfs.id")
[1] TRUE
```

FIGURE 15.   *ORCH metadata file content*

Working with Hadoop Using the ORCH Framework

Using, or not using, a mapper or reducer function in a Hadoop job can produce some useful behaviors. For example, consider a simple MapReduce job to run a piece of R code in parallel on different chunks of HDFS data. In Oracle R Enterprise Embedded R Execution, this corresponds to `ore.rowApply`. In ORCH, users accomplish this by providing a mapper, but using a default reducer that passes the results through. The function `orch.keyvals` (notice the "s") unlists the reducer input and writes it as multiple key values.

```
hadoop.exec(file, mapper={...}, reducer={orch.keyvals(k,vv)})
```

Alternatively, to run R code in parallel on partitions of the data, that is, by HDFS key column, specify only the reducer and use the mapper specified next, which partitions the data. This functionality corresponds to the `ore.groupApply` function.

```
hadoop.exec(file, mapper={orch.keyval(k,v)}, reducer={...})
```

Of course, the full MapReduce functionality is provided for both a mapper and reducer, or further configuring a job with the `config` argument.

```
hadoop.exec(file, mapper={...}, reducer={...})
hadoop.exec(file, mapper={...}, reducer={...}, config={...})
```

MapReduce jobs can be configured using a wide range of fields. A job configuration object is of type `mapred.config` and contains the fields shown in Listing 17 with their default values. Any of these can be overridden as needed. For example, users may want to provide a name for jobs that will show up in standard Hadoop monitoring interfaces. Users may also need to characterize the mapper and reducer output if it is different from the input.

Listing 17 *ORCH MapReduce job configuration*

```
R> jobconfig = new("mapred.config")
R> class(jobconfig)
[1] "mapred.config"
attr(,"package")
[1] ".GlobalEnv"
R> jobconfig
Object of class "mapred.config"
data frame with 0 columns and 0 rows
Slot "job.name":  ←——————— User-defined job name
[1] ""
Slot "map.tasks":  ←——————— Desired #mappers
[1] -1
```

```
Slot "reduce.tasks":  ◄─────── Desired #reducers
[1] -1
Slot "min.split.size":  ◄─────── Desired minimum # rows sent to mapper
[1] -1
Slot "map.output":  ◄─────── Schema of mapper output
data frame with 0 columns and 0 rows
Slot "reduce.output":  ◄─────── Schema of reducer output
data frame with 0 columns and 0 rows
Slot "map.valkey":  ◄─────── Should key be included in mapper value?
[1] FALSE
Slot "reduce.valkey":  ◄─────── Should key be included in reducer value?
[1] FALSE
Slot "map.input":  ◄─────── Data type of val that is input to mapper: data.frame or list
[1] "vector"
Slot "map.split":
[1] 1  ◄─────── Max chunk size desired by mapper
Slot "reduce.input":
[1] "list"  ◄─────── Data type of val that is input to reducer: data.frame or list
Slot "reduce.split":
[1] 0  ◄─────── Max chunk size desired by the reducer - zero indicates no limit
Slot "verbose":
[1] FALSE  ◄─────── Should diagnostic info be generated?
```

ORCH Predictive Analytics on Hadoop

While MapReduce is a powerful programming paradigm and Hadoop a powerful computing environment, not everyone wants to or can write MapReduce programs to harness that power. To make Hadoop-based analytics more accessible, ORCH contains a set of built-in algorithms with a convenient R interface. The underlying algorithms are built on the ORCH framework using MapReduce for scalable, high-performance execution. These R interfaces are generally consistent with typical R predictive analytics functions.

Functions include linear models, low-rank matrix factorization, neural networks, and non-negative matrix factorization, as listed in Table 11.

For an example, consider orch.lm. The function orch.lm is a scalable lm implementation on top of Hadoop, able to process well over a thousand columns of data, with no effective restriction on the number of rows. The result is of class orch.lm and a subclass of lm with corresponding functions print and summary. The orch.lm interface allows a formula specification, as in the lm and ore.lm functions.

In Example 26, the iris data set is used to predict Petal.Width given the cube of the Sepal.Length and the combination of Sepal.Width and Petal.Length. After fitting the model, the fit is printed to display the coefficients for each term. Invoking summary provides output similar to a standard lm model with the min and

Function	Description
orch.lm	Fits a linear model using tall-and-skinny QR (TSQR) factorization and parallel distribution. The function computes the same statistical arguments as the Oracle R Enterprise ore.lm function.
orch.lmf	Fits a low-rank matrix factorization model using either the Jellyfish algorithm or the Mahout alternating least squares with weighted regularization (ALS-WR) algorithm.
orch.neural	Produces a neural network to model complex, nonlinear relationships between inputs and outputs to find patterns in the data.
orch.nmf	Provides the main entry point to create a non-negative matrix factorization model using the Jellyfish algorithm. This function can work on much larger data sets than the R NMF package, because the input does not need to fit into memory.

TABLE 11. *ORCH Analytic Functions*

max of the residuals, and coefficients with standard error, t value, and significance, among other statistics. This is depicted in Listing 18.

Example 26:

```
formula <- 'Petal.Width ~ I(Sepal.Length^3) + (Sepal.Width + Petal.Length)^2'
dfs.dat <- hdfs.put(iris)
fit = orch.lm(formula, dfs.dat)
print(fit)
```

Listing 18 *Results of orch.lm for Example 26*

```
R> print(fit)
Call:
orch.lm(formula = formula, dfs.dat = dfs.dat)
Coefficients:
    (Intercept)    I(Sepal.Length^3)    Sepal.Width    Petal.Length
Sepal.Width:Petal.Length
   -0.558951258        -0.001808531    0.076544835     0.374865543
0.044639138

R> summary(fit)
Call:
```

```
orch.lm(formula = formula, dfs.dat = dfs.dat)
Residuals:
      Min        Max
-0.5787561  0.5982218
Coefficients:
                           Estimate    Std. Error    t value     Pr(>|t|)
(Intercept)              -0.558951258  0.3114271138  -1.7948060  7.476772e-02
I(Sepal.Length^3)        -0.001808531  0.0003719886  -4.8617906  2.990386e-06
Sepal.Width               0.076544835  0.0936509172   0.8173421  4.150739e-01
Petal.Length              0.374865543  0.0813489249   4.6081192  8.829319e-06
Sepal.Width:Petal.Length  0.044639138  0.0244578742   1.8251438  7.003728e-02
Multiple R-squared: 0.9408,     Adjusted R-squared: 0.9392
F-statistic: 576.6 on 4 and 145 DF
```

ORCHhive

Hive is a SQL-like abstraction on top of Hadoop that is becoming a de facto standard for SQL-based apps on Hadoop. It effectively converts SQL queries to MapReduce jobs that are run on the Hadoop cluster. This allows users to write HiveQL, which is based on SQL, to manipulate data without knowledge of MapReduce programming.

So while Hive provides an abstraction layer using SQL syntax on top of MapReduce, ORCHhive provides an R abstraction on top of HiveQL, just as ORE provides an R abstraction on top of SQL. This allows Big Data scalability and performance for R users on Hadoop, but doing so easily and transparently from R. A key motivation for ORCHhive is to allow users to prepare Big Data for further analytic techniques using the ORCH MapReduce framework.

ORCHhive supports a wide range of R functions for transparent interaction with Hive tables. Table 12 includes a list of supported functions from storage methods to methods on primitive types like logical, numeric, and character vectors, as well as `ore.frames` and aggregation functions.

ORCH provides the same ORE functions to work with Hive. Although this is an ORE-like interface, it is a feature available only with ORCH. Consider the ORCHhive R script in Example 27. Users connect to Hive using `ore.connect`, specifying `type="HIVE"`. There are no login credentials since Hadoop does not have authentication. Users simply indicate they are connecting to the local Hive environment. Next, attach the current environment into the R search path using `ore.attach`. The tables in Hive are now available to ORCH. Create a Hive table in HDFS using `ore.push`, using the `iris` data set. The Transparency Layer is highlighted by binning the data using standard R syntax. These operations are performed on Hadoop using Hive tables. As with other `ore.frames`, users can ask for the column names. Lastly, the overloaded `aggregate` function is used to compute summary statistics over each petal length bin created earlier. In the output shown in Listing 19, Large petals have a minimum value of 6 and a maximum value of 6.9.

Storage methods	ore.create, ore.drop, ore.push, ore.pull, ore.get
Methods	is.ore.frame, is.ore.vector, is.ore.logical, is.ore.integer, is.ore.numeric, is.ore.character, is.ore, as.ore.frame, as.ore.vector, as.ore.logical, as.ore.integer, as.ore.numeric, as.ore.character, as.ore
ore.vector methods	show, length, c, is.vector, as.vector, as.character, as.numeric, as.integer, as.logical, "|", "|<-", |, Compare, ore.recode, is.na, "%in%", unique, sort, table, paste, tapply, by, head, tail
ore.logical methods	<, >, ==, <=, >=, !, xor, ifelse, and, or
ore.number methods	+, -, *, ^, %%, %/%, /, is.finite, is.infinite, is.nan, abs, sign, sqrt, ceiling, floor, trunc, log, log10, log2, log1p, logb, acos, asin atan, exp, expm1, cos, sin, tan, zapsmall, round, Summary, summary, mean
ore.character methods	nchar, tolower, toupper, casefold, gsub, substr, substring
ore.frame methods	show, attach, [, $, $<-, [[, [[<-, head, tail, length, nrow, ncol, NROW, NCOL, dim, names, names<-, colnames, colnames<-, as.list, unlist, summary, rbind, cbind, data.frame, as.data.frame, as.env, eval, +, -, *, ^, %%, %/%, /, Compare, Logic, !, xor, is.na, is.finite, is.infinite, is.nan, abs, sign, sqrt, ceiling, floor, trunc, log, log10, log2, log1p, logb, acos, asin, atan, exp, expm1, cos, sin, tan, round, Summary, rowSums, colSums, rowMeans, colMeans, unique, by, merge
Aggregate functions	OREStats: fivenum, aggregate, quantile, sd, var (only for vectors), median, IQR

TABLE 12. *ORCHhive-Supported Functionality*

Example 27:

```
# Connect to Hive
ore.connect(type="HIVE")
# Attach the current environment into search path of R
ore.attach()
# create a Hive table by pushing the numeric columns of the iris data set
IRIS_TABLE <- ore.push(iris[1:4])
# Create bins based on Petal Length
IRIS_TABLE$PetalBins = ifelse(IRIS_TABLE$Petal.Length < 2.0, "SMALL PETALS",
                       ifelse(IRIS_TABLE$Petal.Length < 4.0, "MEDIUM PETALS",
```

```
            ifelse(IRIS_TABLE$Petal.Length < 6.0,
                    "MEDIUM LARGE PETALS", "LARGE PETALS")))
#PetalBins is now a derived column of the HIVE object
names(IRIS_TABLE)
# Based on the bins, generate summary statistics for each group
aggregate(IRIS_TABLE$Petal.Length, by = list(PetalBins = IRIS_TABLE$PetalBins),
        FUN = summary)
```

Listing 19 *Results of executing ORCHhive Example 27*

```
ore.connect(type="HIVE")
ore.attach()
# create a Hive table by pushing the numeric
# columns of the iris data set
IRIS_TABLE <- ore.push(iris[1:4])
# Create bins based on Petal Length
 IRIS_TABLE$PetalBins =
    ifelse(IRIS_TABLE$Petal.Length < 2.0, "SMALL PETALS",
+    ifelse(IRIS_TABLE$Petal.Length < 4.0, "MEDIUM PETALS",
+    ifelse(IRIS_TABLE$Petal.Length < 6.0,
+    "MEDIUM LARGE PETALS", "LARGE PETALS")))
ore.connect(type="HIVE")
ore.attach()
# create a Hive table by pushing the numeric
# columns of the iris data set
IRIS_TABLE <- ore.push(iris[1:4])
# Create bins based on Petal Length
 IRIS_TABLE$PetalBins =
    ifelse(IRIS_TABLE$Petal.Length < 2.0, "SMALL PETALS",
+    ifelse(IRIS_TABLE$Petal.Length < 4.0, "MEDIUM PETALS",
+    ifelse(IRIS_TABLE$Petal.Length < 6.0,
+    "MEDIUM LARGE PETALS", "LARGE PETALS")))

#PetalBins is now a derived column of the HIVE object
> names(IRIS_TABLE)
[1] "Sepal.Length" "Sepal.Width"  "Petal.Length"
[4] "Petal.Width"  "PetalBins"

# Based on the bins, generate summary statistics for each group
aggregate(IRIS_TABLE$Petal.Length,
        by = list(PetalBins = IRIS_TABLE$PetalBins),
+          FUN = summary)
1          LARGE PETALS    6 6.025000 6.200000 6.354545 6.612500   6.9 0
2 MEDIUM LARGE PETALS    4 4.418750 4.820000 4.888462 5.275000   5.9 0
3         MEDIUM PETALS    3 3.262500 3.550000 3.581818 3.808333   3.9 0
4         SMALL PETALS    1 1.311538 1.407692 1.462000 1.507143   1.9 0
Warning message:
ORE object has no unique key - using random order
```

ORCH and ORE Interaction

ORCH and ORE can be combined in a variety of ways to solve interesting problems. If ORE and ORCH are installed on a user's client machine, not only can data be moved between HDFS and the database, but also preprocessed database data can be provided to MapReduce jobs. Similarly, results from MapReduce jobs can be post-processed in the database once data is moved there.

For example, a CUSTOMER table may reside in Oracle Database and require cleaning or aggregation prior to use by a MapReduce job that makes a wide range of recommendations for those customers. These recommendations could be produced by scoring hundreds or thousands of models per customer, where the models were generated using ORE and stored in an ORE datastore, only to be retrieved and passed into ORCH as exported variables.

In another configuration, ORE can be installed on Big Data Appliance (BDA) task nodes such that mapper and reducer functions can make call-outs to one or more databases for ORE-based processing, using the Transparency Layer or Embedded R Execution.

Conversely, ORCH can be installed on the Oracle Database server such that Embedded R Execution can invoke ORCH functionality. One immediate use is the scheduling of database jobs for recurring execution. Here, the database can control when and how often ORCH MapReduce jobs get executed as part of a database application.

Summary

Oracle R Enterprise provides a comprehensive, database-centric environment for end-to-end analytical processes in R. Both the results of R script execution and the R scripts themselves can be immediately deployed to production environments. Oracle R Enterprise improves user efficiency by allowing the use of R directly against database data, and leveraging in-database analytical techniques. Using Oracle Database as a computational engine provides scalability and performance through in-database execution, query optimization, parallelism, and elimination of data movement. The rich set of open source R packages can be used in combination with database-managed data-parallel and task-parallel execution of R scripts— leveraging Oracle Database as a high-performance computing (HPC) environment. As a result, ORE provides a framework for sophisticated model building and data scoring. By integrating R into the SQL language, operationalization of analyst-generated R scripts enables more immediate integration with the IT software stack.

ORCH allows R users to leverage the powerful Hadoop environment from R. Both mapper and reducer functions are written using the R language and environment. The ORCH HDFS interface facilitates access to database data, file-based data, and R `data.frames`. Using the dry run capability, R-based MapReduce jobs can be tested and debugged in the local system prior to unleashing a newly written program on the full Hadoop cluster. ORCH provides a number of advanced analytics algorithms that make it easy for users to gain Hadoop scalability for commonly used techniques. In addition, users can manipulate HIVE data transparently from R using familiar R syntax and semantics.

Oracle customers have the added benefit of using Oracle R Distribution, which provides, among other benefits, Oracle support, making R a viable option for world-class enterprises.

Conclusion

This concludes our short book on Oracle's R products and technologies. We hope you will find the contents useful should your organization implement R in the future. Due to space and time constraints, we could not cover every topic, but tried to cover the most important ones.

If you have enjoyed this book, we would encourage you to take a look at the companion book, *Oracle Big Data Handbook*, also published by Oracle Press.

As well as covering the earlier topics on R, *Oracle Big Data Handbook* includes coverage of the following topics:

- Introduction to Big Data

- The Value of Big Data

- The Apache Hadoop Platform

- Why an Appliance?

- BDA Configurations, Deployment Architectures, and Monitoring

- Integrating the Data Warehouse and Analytics Infrastructure to Big Data

- BDA Connectors

- Oracle NoSQL Database

- In-database Analytics: Delivering Faster Time to Value

- Analyzing Data with R

- Endeca Information Discovery

- Big Data Governance

- Developing Architecture and Roadmap for Big Data

Oracle Big Data Handbook represents two years of work by the leading Big Data experts at Oracle and was written by Tom Plunkett, Brian Macdonald, Bruce Nelson, Helen Sun, Mark F. Hornick, Keith Laker, Khader Mohiuddin, Debra L. Harding, David Segleau, Gokula Mishra, and Robert Stackowiak, with the same technical editor team of Jean-Pierre Dijcks and Dan McClary.

That's it for now. Thank you for choosing this book, and we wish you the best of luck in your work with R.

Exercises

1. Describe four problems enterprises encounter when working with open source R and enterprise data.

2. Compare and contrast the features of three open source R GUIs or IDEs.

3. Name three benefits provided by the ORE Transparency Layer.

4. How does the ORE Transparency Layer achieve each of the benefits identified in Exercise 3?

5. Which open source R database interface package would you choose and why?

6. What features of ORE allow R graphs to be displayed in dashboard tools, such as OBIEE?

7. Why would an enterprise want to use Oracle R Distribution over open source R?

8. What are the three computational engines leveraged by ORE and how do they interact?

9. How is application architecture affected when transitioning from a file-based solution to a database-based solution?

10. When connecting to Oracle Database, in what situations should you use `ore.sync` and `ore.attach` over setting the `all` argument of `ore.connect` to TRUE?

11. Using the R data set `mtcars`, write R code that demonstrates creating an `ore.frame` object and selecting the names of cars with miles per gallon greater than 20 and weight greater than 3.

12. From a hypothetical database table TAB_1 with 1000 columns named C1..C1000, write the R code that produces an `ore.frame` excluding columns C100 through C110 and C1000.

13. Using database tables TAB_1 with columns A, B, C; TAB_2 with columns A, D, F; and TAB_3 with columns F, G, H, write R code to join these tables such that *all* data from the tables will be included in the result. Ensure that the resulting ore.frame has only one column with each letter, and that column names are in alphabetical order. Hint: Use outer joins.

14. Using the R mtcars data set, create a temporary ore.frame object, build a linear model to predict miles per gallon using the R data.frame, and build a Support Vector Machine model using ore.odmSVM to predict weight on the ore.frame. Then, create a datastore to persist these. Show the output of executing ore.datastore and ore.datastoreSummary on the datastore created.

15. Create a synthetic time series data.frame with columns x and y, where x ranges from Sys.Date() to 500 days in the past, and y ranges from 1 to 500 with a random normal component (be creative). Push this data.frame to the database. Select rows between the 10 percent and 25 percent quantiles. Build an ARIMA model and plot the results.

16. Using the R iris data set, produce train and test stratified samples of the data. Ensure that there is a balanced number of each "Species" in the train and test sets.

17. Describe four benefits of using ORE Embedded R Execution and two limitations.

18. List the Embedded R Execution functions in the R interface and describe under which conditions each might be used.

19. Define a function *f* for use with ore.indexApply that computes summary on one column of an ore.frame, selected based on the index provided as argument to *f*. Store *f* in the R script repository using ore.scriptCreate and invoke using ore.indexApply using the iris data set.

20. Define a function *f* for use with rqTableEval that takes a data set of your choice, builds an lm model where the formula is specified as an argument to *f*, generates images using plot on the lm model, and returns the model. Describe the differences in results when the return type is changed among NULL, 'XML', and 'PNG'.

21. Compare the performance difference between building predictive models when using R models versus in-database models. Select a large (100k+) data set suitable for modeling and load it into Oracle Database using ore.create. For R, time the execution of ore.pull along with the model build time for {e1071} naivebayes and svm, {stats} lm, and {rpart} rpart. For ORE, time the execution of ore.odmNB, ore.odmSVM, ore.lm, and ore.odmDT. Do the same for scoring data with the resulting models. Choose additional algorithms for comparison as extra credit.

22. Using the `rpart` model produced in the previous exercise, use `ore`
    `.predict` to score data with this model in the database. Compare the
    execution time of scoring in R and writing results to the database (using
    `ore.create`) with `ore.predict`.

23. Describe four benefits associated with Oracle R Connector for Hadoop.

24. In ORCH, write a MapReduce job using `hadoop.exec` to score data in a
    row-parallel manner. The predictive model used for scoring will have been
    created locally in R, for example, using `lm`, and made available to each
    mapper and/or reducer. (Hint: Use `orch.export`.)

25. Select a data set to test the MapReduce job in Exercise 24. Load the data
    into HDFS either from Oracle Database, the file system, or R `data.frame`.
    Execute the MapReduce job in dry run mode first. Then execute on the
    Hadoop cluster.

26. Describe how ORCHhive is both similar to and different from ORE.

Useful Links

- Comprehensive R Archive Network (CRAN), http://cran.us.r-project.org/

- CRAN Task Views, http://cran.r-project.org/web/views/

- CRAN Books related to R, www.r-project.org/doc/bib/R-books.html

- crantastic, http://crantastic.org/

- Hadoop, http://hadoop.apache.org/

- Hive, http://hive.apache.org/

- Machine Learning CRAN Task View, http://cran.r-project.org/web/views/
  MachineLearning.html

- Oracle Advanced Analytics, www.oracle.com/us/products/database/options/
  advanced-analytics

- Oracle BI Publisher, www.oracle.com/technetwork/middleware/bi-publisher

- Oracle Big Data Connectors, www.oracle.com/us/products/database/
  big-data-connectors

■ Oracle Business Intelligence Enterprise Edition, www.oracle.com/us/solutions/business-analytics/business-intelligence/enterprise-edition

■ Oracle Data Mining, www.oracle.com/technetwork/database/options/advanced-analytics/odm

■ Oracle Database, www.oracle.com/us/products/database

■ Oracle DBMS_SCHEDULER, http://docs.oracle.com/cd/E11882_01/appdev.112/e16760/d_sched.htm

■ Oracle R Blog, https://blogs.oracle.com/r

■ Oracle R Distribution, www.oracle.com/technetwork/indexes/downloads/r-distribution-1532464.html

■ Oracle R Enterprise, www.oracle.com/technetwork/database/options/advanced-analytics/r-enterprise

■ R Commander, www.rcommander.com/

■ R Graph Gallery, http://gallery.r-enthusiasts.com/

■ R Language Definition, http://cran.r-project.org/doc/manuals/r-release/R-lang.html

■ Rattle, http://cran.r-project.org/web/packages/rattle

■ ROracle Package, http://cran.r-project.org/web/packages/ROracle/index.html

■ RStudio, www.rstudio.com

CPSIA information can be obtained at www.ICGtesting.com
Printed in the USA
LVOW11s0426290414

383639LV00006B/99/P